Woodworking Tools

Also by Frederick Oughton

The finishing and re-finishing of wood (1969)

Woodworking Tools

Frederick Oughton,
Fellow of the Royal Society of Arts

Constable London

First published in Great Britain 1973
by Constable & Company Ltd
10 Orange Street, London WC2H 7EG
Copyright © 1973 by Frederick Oughton

ISBN 0 09 458210 6

Set in Photon Times
Printed in Great Britain by
Alden & Mowbray Ltd
at the Alden Press, Oxford

For Ruth and Rhian

Contents

Illustrations

Foreword

If you are one of those people who knows very little about woodworking tools, you probably think that any chisel, hammer or screwdriver will do for any job. Most people are casual about such things—and it probably explains the number of botched do-it-yourself jobs you come across in other people's houses. Of course, you would be flabbergasted if your dentist tried to extract a tooth with a drill. And we would think a bricklayer was mad if he tried to build a wall with an awl. But lots of people cheerfully think nothing at all about trying to shove a three-inch screw into a piece of oak, using a ground-down chisel or even the end of the wife's nail file. It is only when you are sitting in the casualty department, waiting for somebody to bandage your gashed hand that it dawns on you that something went wrong . . .

Craftsmen are very fussy about tools. That's natural enough, because they are one of the few guilds who, at the end of the apprenticeship lasting between five and seven years, buy their own tools and look after them for up to half a century of working life. Time was when they made their own tools to such a degree of perfection that these same tools, now up to a couple of centuries old, fetch high prices as collector's pieces.

An engineer's wrench is nothing more than an instrument for gripping and holding nuts and bolts or lengths of piping. But a wood chisel is a true union between the skilled craftsman in wood and his materials. The wrench is simply tightened and turned. A chisel leads the way.

As a lad my ebullient nature was held in check by my stepfather who would detail me to do the paint scraping, creosoting and cleaning out of the henhouses. But my stepfather was always worried that I would damage his prized collection of woodworking tools, many of which had been in his family of yeoman farmers for more than a century. Looking back, I don't blame him, because he had a true craftsman's instinct . . . although I must admit that I had to stifle my youthful criticism of a kind of Noah's Ark of a wheelbarrow which he knocked up out of scrap timber and part of an old railway sleeper. The wheel itself was vaguely circular. At the christening ceremony, which mother and I attended with our pint mugs of tea, it took a person of some brawn and brutal strength to get the vehicle moving at all. As Joseph, my stepfather, was only about five foot something or other, the wheelbarrow spent most of its days near the muckheap, a monument to its own robust construction, with elaborate joints and nuts and bolts strong enough to secure the plates of an ocean liner. Still, it was an object lesson in the proper use of tools. I am not quite sure what happened to it in the end. After Joseph's death my mother probably called in the demolition squad. So you can see that my apprenticeship consisted mainly of standing and watching.

Ever since those past days of long hot summers I have appreciated Joseph's law that I must keep my fingers out of his tool chest. The same goes for most craftsmen. And as for lending tools out—well, it's like parting with your own limbs. At the same time, there seems to be a dearth of dads who nowadays do what Joseph eventually did for me and buy their lads—and daughters too!—a set of tools. We talk enough about the problems of youth and we should by now know that their real problem is one of finding something to do.

From the other side of the fence, a lot of husbands object to their wives borrowing even a hammer and nail, and I have known a kind of civil war to go on between neighbours when one of them borrows a plane or a saw and is then thoughtless enough to bring it back damaged. The chap down the road can have the shirt off my back, but I'm damned if he can have a loan of the spokeshave I've used for so many years.

I was demonstrating wood carving and sculpture at a big London exhibition some time ago and I had to answer one question after another about tools and wood. One of them came from a prison officer who said he had been trying to start carving classes for prisoners. But he was hampered because he had no money to spend, so he loaned out his own carving tools. Anybody who knows anything about carving

tools knows how delicate they are and what a nuisance
they are to sharpen satisfactorily. I told him he ought
to have a medal from the Prison Commissioners.

What I have tried to do is tell you not only about
the woodworking tools themselves, but something
about their qualities and the way they work, also
something about their history. Lots of tools have
changed very little since they were first introduced, but
others have come to fruition in devious ways, dictated
by the needs of craftsmen. Some tools were invented
for one particular kind of job, but over a period of two
centuries or so they have been modified so that nowadays they do quite a different job. If you want to
know something about the lineage of tools, it is worth
visiting the Victoria and Albert Museum, London,
where they have a large collection of them.

There is another reason for this book: I hope to
persuade you that it is stupid to go buying tools unless
you know what to look out for. There is a certain type
of screwdriver fitted with a patent chuck and a hollow
handle which contains up to a dozen different widths
of screwdriver bits, tools for making holes and other
tools for countersinking screws. I squirm when I read
the makers' claim that this tool is a miniature
workshop. They seem to have overlooked the fact that
the handle is too fat to hold comfortably and,
furthermore, the securing cap (plastic) tends to come
off while you are screwing. The best person to design
tools is the craftsman rather than the theorist.

That brings us to the question of who actually

designs tools in the first place. Apart from the patent gadgets which pop up every year and are forgotten within months, the ordinary traditional tools have designed themselves. They are links in a chain of technical evolution, and we are now at a point where all the principles are so well known that it is practically impossible to invent a perfectly new screwdriver, hammer or saw. After all, the idea of having a thicker or thinner handle or a longer or shorter shaft is just a matter of personal preference. You can have a lot of fun, trying to improve the screwdriver, but you will always come back to first principles.

The tool-using fraternity is very conservative, and although it may be gadget conscious to a certain extent, no manufacturer has yet managed to create a runaway success with an item like the 'universal tool' which reams, rebates, chamfers and gives your toenails a polish at the same time, for few of these gadgets last for long. Some of the less reputable manufacturers seem to think that a built-in obsolescence is the road to bigger and better sales, but they have misjudged a consumer-conscious society. The needs of the average buyer of tools shows a middle-aged man who can just about muster a few pennies a week for new tools. He saves up for what he wants or else he gets them on credit. This sort of buying demands value for money. If the fellow cannot get value, he will spend the money on other things. A couple of examples will tell you what I mean.

I wanted a small soldering iron, so I bought one from a tool shop, and it was imported from Canada. I must admit it looked pretty smart in its bubble pack. As soon as I pierced the bubble, I discovered that the ceramic collar was cracked. It fell to pieces when I pulled the iron out. The shop would not exchange it for a new one, but they offered to show it to the firm's representative 'in about a week when he calls in'. A fortnight later I called in. The representative had not been near the place. This game went on for two months. I was angry and embarrassed at the same time, so I said: 'Let's forget it, shall we? You hang on to my soldering iron and keep my money.' I was quickly given a new soldering iron.

The second story about bad 'toolmanship' involved an electric bandsaw, widely promoted and nationally advertised. It looked good to me, so I thought I would buy one and save a lot of my labour. A reliable bandsaw would save cussing and sweating. So I plunged. I sent off the order and a cheque with it, and when it arrived I found that it was defective. It broke its blades, it would not cut putty without something going wrong. This made nonsense of the manufacturer's claim that it would saw three-inch hardwood. They gladly sent me some replacement saws free of charge, first one at a time and then three or four in each carton. Four weeks and a lot of written complaints later, they sent me a brand new machine. But this one also had faults. By this time I was eating, sleeping and dreaming the damned bandsaw, and I was pretty sure there must be something wrong with the design of the thing, and so I sent a full report to the manufacturers. They liked my report. They congratulated me on my helpfulness. In the meantime they ensured that I received an almost unlimited supply of free blades, all of which broke, because of inferior butt welding.

One day they phoned me right out of the blue to announce that they were now modifying a machine for my special use. It was delivered and I plugged in. But it was much worse than the other two bandsaws. At the time of writing I am the possessor of three bandsaws, all of them defective one way or another, and I have gone back to hand sawing.

Spending money on good tools is not as hazardous as it might seem. If you do have a breakage or the tool develops some other fault within a reasonable time of purchase, most of the well known makers will replace it or repair it free of charge, and they will probably refund your postage into the bargain. I once snapped a carbon steel carving gouge. I thought that it might have been one of a batch of tools made from faulty steel, so I wrote to the manufacturer to warn him. Within four days they sent me a brand new gouge and a courteous letter.

There is, for instance, the firm which offers 'brand new and unused ex-Army toolsets' at half the market price. What they don't tell you is that the tools are coated with rust after spending more than twenty years in damp stores. In one case the drills were so badly

corroded that to use them in a power drill might have
meant the loss of an eye or a chunk of metal embedded
in your flesh. Any metal which revolves at high speed
will create a build-up of frictional heat and, ultimately,
metal fatigue. This, in turn, can make it disintegrate,
throwing off pieces of metal with the velocity of
bullets. It happens without warning in less than a
second. It is not hard to see the kind of tragedy which
might happen if a child is standing nearby. It is
unfortunately very difficult to get hold of precise
information or statistics about this type of accident,
but we do know that the number of domestic accidents
which happen every year rival the number of accidents
on the roads. The exact nature of the accidents is
hidden away in the statistics, but my own guess is that
a lot of them are caused by faulty tools of all kinds.
That is one of the two reasons why I have written this
book. The other reason is that I thought there was a
need for it.

A very special word of thanks is due to Messrs J. E.
Ware, J. McNally and J. D. Green of Wolf Electric
Tools Limited for all the time and trouble they went
to, and for the supply of equipment, which went far
beyond my expectations. I extend my grateful thanks
to Aven Tools Limited for bringing their new ranges to
my attention, and to Mr E. R. Baumeister and Mr B.
W. Hannan for useful information about bandsaws. I
am especially grateful to Mr R. A. Brown of Stanley-
Bridges Limited for practical assistance in the matter

of the Stanley 267 Router; to Mr D. M. Short of Stanley Works Limited for advice and practical assistance throughout the gestation of this book; to Mr J. M. Warwick Pridham of R. Parramore and Sons Limited, who gave his expert assistance with the Paramo Planemaster, G-cramps and bench vices; and to Mr R. Johnson of Myford Limited for information about multi-purpose woodworking machinery. Amongst the pioneers of good new ideas I am indebted to Mr R. P. Hickman for material about the Workmate portable workbench. Castinali Products provided data on a unique dowelling jig. Mr J. A. Sainsbury of C. and J. Hampton Limited was very encouraging and helpful on the subject of hand tool selection. And, lastly, I would like to thank two personal craftsmen friends who weighed in with their own hints and tips, namely Ken Jones of Anglesey—in the course of our talks he has taught me a great deal about tools and their qualities—and Gino Masero, master carver and artist, with whom I have shared many an exploration and will share more in the years to come.

London, 1973   Frederick Oughton

1 Rummaging in the toolchest

What is the life of tools? I have used some over a century old. Those used by Grinling Gibbons between December 1694 and March 1695 to carve what he called in his invoice '2 Boyes 3 ft. high in wanscot and the Urne'* for £14, might still be in existence. Good tools can enjoy a very long life. Bad tools soon get on your nerves and so you chuck them away. Lieutenant Colonel Ronald A. Cox, the Scottish craftsman, recently presented me with twenty-two tools which he found in a Highland village. Long before the First World War it was famous as a woodworking and carving centre, and the tools are now putting in some more service on my own bench. Their steel has what I can only call a satin look, they sharpen quickly and hold their edge. No wonder such things are so much sought after, not only by the modern craftsmen but also by collectors and museums throughout the world. That is why you keep hearing the old lament: 'They'll never make them like this again.' Steel made before 1914 was certainly superior

* If you are interested in the great Grinling Gibbons, I can recommend the book, *Grinling Gibbons—His Work as Carver and Statuary, 1648–1721,* by David Bronte Green (Country Life, 1964).

to anything that rolls off the modern assembly line. You can prove this by taking an old chisel and a modern one and sharpening them on the same stone, then using them on identical woods. In no time the modern one will need re-sharpening while the old one will remain as sharp as ever. Modern steel seems to be brittle and the edges chip very easily, needing a lot of care and attention. But despite my disparaging remarks, a good quality edged tool should give between fifteen and twenty years' service. If you do come across pre-1914 tools, they are worth £5 or more apiece. There must be many widows of old carpenters with a small fortune sitting in that old toolchest up in the attic.

If you want to buy a full toolchest nowadays you find yourself faced with problems of choice, and while all you really need are the essentials, your best plan is to start with a saw, chisel, screwdriver and hammer. But there always seems to be something else you might need. So what you should do first of all is sit down and make a list. But don't get the whole family in on the act. Do it yourself, because opinions about what you need will always differ. Of course, a lot depends on the sort of work you want to do. If it is a matter of window frames and doors, you will need tools for setting corners and angles. What I have tried to do in the following list is cover tools which come in handy for all kinds of jobs—a real utility set, in fact.

24 inch hand saw

10 inch tenon saw

Plane

Ratchet brace

Auger bits

Bradawls

No. 2 claw hammer

Carpenter's square

Pincers

Pliers

Spokeshave

Boxwood folding rule

Beechwood mallet

$\frac{1}{4}$—1 inch firmer chisels

Screwdrivers

Marking and mortice gauge

Cork rubber, glass paper

Nail sets

Pin hammer

Half-round files, rasps, etc.

Saw files

Carpenter's pencil

At the time of writing it is practically impossible to provide even a guide to prices, because of the lightning inflation which plays ducks and drakes with ideas of what tools are really worth. In recent months a 20 oz. claw hammer which used to cost less than £1 has gone up to £1·25. I guess that for all the tools on my list you could reckon to pay up to £20. If this seems high, bear in mind that it offers a better investment than anything the unit trusts can give you. Spend as much as you can afford on the basic tools and don't waste money on rubbish.

If good tools are necessary, then so is the bench which completes the woodworking unit. The bench has a very long lineage, stretching way back to the Romans. They developed the plane, and it was this that made it necessary to make something better than

the trestle workhorse which had been in use ever since
wood was first worked. When you analyse the bench it
turns out to be nothing more nor less than a table; a
place where the job can be held tightly while it is being
worked. The primary requirement is that it shall have
complete stability, be of sufficient width and stand at
the right height. When I was in Sicily I knew a dwarf
carpenter. Now, I am about 5 ft 10 in. and he just
about reached up to my waist. His bench was only 2 ft
8 in. high and he had to work standing on a stool until
I one day suggested that he saw a foot off the four feet
of the bench legs. He had been a carpenter for more
than twenty years, but the idea of mutilating the bench
enraged him. Before the war, when I was in the
Merchant Navy, I often sat and watched the ship's
chippy working at a portable bench which he had
designed and built for his own use, basing the design
on a German bench of 1505, using bench pegs which
would hold almost any size of workpiece. The whole
thing could be knocked down and fitted into a smart
mahogany chest embellished with brass corners and a
handle studded with pieces of polished malachite.

So obviously everything must depend on where and
how you want to work. A bench located in a garage or
a shed might be subject to damp, and if it is fitted with
tool drawers and a cupboard for the inevitable odds
and ends, they will probably stick. I know that some of
the purists will throw up their hands in horror at the
idea of drawers and cupboards, because the
traditionalists generally store odd lengths of timber

underneath the bench. All the same, storage space is important nowadays, when so many of us are cooped up in tower blocks. Drawers and cupboards are important, otherwise hammers, screwdrivers and planes will find their way into the airing cupboard. The ideal thing is to own a compact bench and storage unit—if only for the safety of the children.

Although benches come in all sizes, a standard set of dimensions can run from 4 ft 4 in. to a middle size of 4 ft 6 in. or, at the outside, 5 ft or 6 ft. You could practically build a battleship on a 6 ft bench, and I don't see much point in having a big one simply because it is the biggest. The standard width of a bench is 2 ft, and the height should be 2 ft 8 in. The plates and the underframes should be made from steamed and well-seasoned beech, which is a traditional wood for this kind of construction. Of course, you can always make a bench to your own design, taking into account that the standard bench is the best one. All you really need is a long flat surface, some bench stops which can be adjusted as the need arises, and one or more vices or holdfasts. Gino Masero, the London master carver who knows a good bench when he sees one, tells me that he had one made by a joinery firm for between £30 and £40, which seems reasonable enough. Another friend made his own bench, using for the top a couple of railway sleepers which can be bought for as little as 50 pence apiece. Of course, once this was placed in position and bolted to the floor and the wall with three-inch carriage bolts, it was virtually irremovable, and when he sold the house he was forced to throw in the bench because it could not be taken out.

Most of us are now design conscious—and a good thing, too—and while you might need a good solid bench to produce good solid work, there is still a need for the bench to look good. A railway sleeper is not so good to look at and you could not, of course, have it standing in the lounge. The possibility of having a bench that can live in the lounge has been strikingly solved by Sjoberg, a Swedish firm.*

I use a Sjoberg and when I got it, I thought it almost too beautiful to use. Once the top was scored and marked by usage, I could have wept. While the Sjoberg is original in design, it has its roots in the German joiner's bench of about 1877 with different arrangements of vices. The end vice of the Sjoberg is particularly useful, because it is used in conjunction with the bench dogs, and there is a back-well to catch shavings and chippings and it can also hold the tools you are using.

The great bench controversy can be argued from different sides, because it all depends what you want to do. Those who want to fake Chippendale for a living or fabricate chair and settee carcases will be happy with a bench which is fixed in one position in the workshop. But the wandering worker who tends to

*The UK agents for Sjoberg are J. Meecham Associates, 15 Kinnaird Avenue, Bromley, Kent.

assemble his tools around him at the place where the job is required soon gets tired of humping trestles and work-horses around with him. If you are building fittings for that little room at the top of the house, it is no joke trying to force sawing trestles through narrow doorways and then bring them down again. As far as I am concerned, the best solution to date is a portable workbench called the Workmate,* which operates on the basis of two vice handles, two clamp knobs and a foot adjuster to twiddle. The top is 27 in. long and it forms a taper vice from 0–3 in. with a parallel or taper motion. The Workmate is stressed like a lady's corset, 36 ways, and I estimate that a medium-sized elephant could sit down on it without causing any anxiety to the owner. It is nine inches lower than ordinary benches, so this makes it especially useful for handling bulky articles like doors and panels, and you can make it even more useful by the use of cramps and other holding devices.

The problem of holding work in progress is divided equally between small and large pieces. In the case of small workpieces, like shelves and little bits of furniture, the vice is an obvious choice, and it should form an integral part of the bench. In my younger and more gipsy-like days, when the sun shone hot, I had a portable vice with a 6 in. jaw and it cost only 35 shillings, holding workpieces of great bulk and weight

* Mate Tools Limited, Brewery Road, Hoddesdon, Hertfordshire, marketed by Black and Decker Limited.

to the detriment of the underside of our kitchen table
on which it was clamped. It was only a light vice, and
if your bench is permanent and you intend using it for
a wide range of work, then the heavier type of vice is
obviously best, such as the Paramo Quick Release
Woodworkers' Vice* with a 7 in., 9 in., or $10\frac{1}{2}$ in. jaw.

A lot of useful holding can be done with G-cramps.
They are obtainable in a range of sizes suitable for
holding a set of false teeth or a sideboard (almost),
from 2 in. to 12 in. I have a liking for cramps, because
they can be manipulated into almost any position,
providing they can get some purchase, and they will
often hold work which is beyond the capacity of the
ordinary vice. When you buy cramps you should not
do as a friend of mine did and magnificently order 'one
of each'. It gave his bank account a ripe old blush,
because the tool factors despatched not only
woodworking cramps but also engineer's cramps, the
cramps used in shipbuilding and others with uses we
never clearly understood. In the ordinary workshop all
you need is a few conventional cramps, because they
will be used for holding work on the bench, securing
the corners of mitred picture frames while you wait for
the glue to set, and one or two general utility cramps.
Although cramps are made for hand pressure, a lot of
amateurs think that hammering the adjustment for
greater tightness will get better results This usually

* F. Parramore and Sons Limited, Caledonian Works,
Chapeltown, Sheffield, S30 4WZ.

results in a cracked workpiece and much annoyance. There is an ancient formula which shows that the strain is governed by the throat depth of the cramp. Obviously, you don't use a 6 in. cramp just to hold a 1 in. piece of moulding in position.

The Workmate, a patent portable folding workbench, incorporating a 0–3 in. parallel and taper vice

An alternative to using cramps is the bench holdfast, which is particularly useful for small workpieces. Holdfasts are made in two sizes of maximum reach, $5\frac{7}{8}$ in. and $7\frac{1}{16}$ in. with maximum openings of $6\frac{7}{8}$ in. and $7\frac{5}{8}$ in. In the great days of cabinet making, when men like Chippendale and Heppelwhite were publishing their pattern books and inviting poor imitations, the cramp was not used at all in cabinet making, because the workpiece was secured by the bench holdfast. To this day many of the older craftsmen use the same method. Only a few days ago I examined two large sideboards in Brecon Cathedral and found signs of the method having been used on the sides of the carved panels. They were made in the Middle Ages, using black oak. Now and then, when carving a small relief panel for a customer, I have noticed the need for constant manipulation, but the bench holdfast tends to be clumsy and tedious, so all I do is cut three battens which stand slightly lower than the workpiece. The battens are secured with nails or screws to the bench top so that the job can be slipped in and out as required. I know at least one craftsman who carves his relief panels on a kind of easel, especially when the work is of a delicate nature, although I prefer to work looking straight down while perched on an adjustable stool. Many relief panels are nowadays made in sections and then glued together, a practice which started in medieval times when a dozen or more craftsmen might be scattered round the country, all working on the same job. It led to some odd variations, of course, such as the multi-layered screen which, when viewed from only a few feet away, looks so intricate as to be beyond even the most accomplished craftsman. It is a gentle deception which cannot be detected unless you examine the edges, where the different layers can be seen, laminated together, held by strong animal glue. A lot of the pierced screens seen in cathedrals were made by this method.

One of the biggest bugbears of joinery is learning how to make accurate and lasting joints, especially when you are trying to put together some simple furniture for the home to save money. Despite the fact that 'woodwork' has always featured in the schoolwork syllabus, about four out of every five of us still do not know how to make a good joint. It just shows how bad our educational system is.

It is in the way of things that somebody somewhere should suddenly hit on the idea of designing a jig to make literally any kind of joint—dovetail, double corner, housing halved, tee bridle, mitre with half lap, angled halving, mitre and mortise and tenon. It has been tried on fourteen-year-old schoolgirls without previous experience of woodwork, it has been used by craftsmen—the most critical breed in the world. Amongst other things, it consists of a cast metal base plate, saw guide pillars, an adjustable bracket, and a wedge. In fact, it is the kind of tool which you might be able to slide into your duffelcoat pocket, probably tearing the fabric in the process. It is that sort of size.

The Jointmaster, a foolproof jig for the precision cutting and making of the full range of joints

The main usefulness of the Jointmaster, which is manufactured and marketed by Copydex Ltd., 1 Torquay Street, Harrow Road, London W2 5BR, is that you can cut as many joints as you like once the jig is set. All you need do is insert a dowel in the appropriate 45 degree hole in the baseplate, the wood being laid against it and the rear saw pillar. Sawing is done with a 12-inch tenon or back saw with a blade at least 3 inches deep, or a 22 inch hand saw with nine teeth to the inch, having small set on the teeth. Making joints with the Jointmaster beats glueing ... although there is a lot to be said for most of the modern adhesives.

Some adhesives will stick wild stallions together. Industrial chemistry has given us many adhesives which do not need protracted pressures to make them work, and we have others which set and harden more gradually to form a virtually unbreakable bond. It can be fun to stick together odd pieces of wood of different kinds and then make small pieces of furniture or use it for turning purposes on a lathe. This goes for wood carving, too, because good quality and well seasoned wood is hard to find.

The adhesives in common use include casein, which is mixed with water. It is probably the cheapest of all glues, and they use it in the furniture trade, and while its effective life varies, you can count on a casein bond lasting for up to twenty-five years. Then there are the contact adhesives, which do what their name suggests. If both surfaces are perfectly clean and dry, you can achieve a bond of about 500 lb psi. The biggest drawback to using contact adhesive is that if you do happen to put two pieces together and leave them for the required time, then change your mind, you will find yourself in queer street, because short of sawing them apart there is no method of breaking the bond.

It goes without saying that a joint should first be tested before it comes within licking distance of an adhesive. This is best done by placing a piece of strong paper in the joint. If a good strong pull results in the paper tearing, the joint is fit for final bonding. If it slips straight out, you will end up with a loose joint.

I do not favour contact adhesives where delicate joints have to be secured. The slower adhesives are to be preferred, such as hide glue, which can withstand 1 ton psi. You first of all soften it in water and then prepare it in a double boiler. The best time to do it is when your wife is out and make sure you open all the windows. It hardens fairly rapidly and it gives you a certain amount of time for manipulation.

While other people would probably put the moon landings down as a twentieth century landmark, I would stick to the synthetic resins, which have tremendous strength.* One example of their use is in some of the stairs at the Festival Hall, London. They

* General and specific information can be obtained from CIBA (A.R.L.) Limited, Duxford, Cambridge. They also issue useful free bulletins.

are made from a patent wood product, Hydulignum,* bonded with resorcinol resin glues. They are so tough that the joints can be immersed in boiling water for prolonged periods without any danger of disintegration or softening. The Festival Hall stairs have been in constant use for more than sixteen years and they show no signs of weakening. Indeed, the last time I was there I jumped my fourteen-and-a-half stone up and down on them when the attendants were looking elsewhere, and my impacted weight did not cause the slightest shudder or vibration. At Ballycastle, Northern Ireland, they made a 210 ft Colombian pine footbridge and used resorcinol glue.

Epoxy glue is another cousin in the same family, and it is made by mixing two parts together, resulting in a bond which can withstand 2 tons psi. As it takes up to twenty-four hours to set and harden, there is ample manipulation time during the first four hours or so.

I have often made use of the simple polyvinyl acetate glue, which is white and creamy, but becomes transparent when it sets. It is useful for mending things like wooden toys. When I finally die I would like to have a bottle of the stuff placed in my coffin, because it did save my life on one occasion. I was demonstrating the use of tools at a trade exhibition in London and I happened to use a chisel with more enthusiasm than

---

* Manufactured by Hordern-Richmond Limited, Gloucester.

attention to the job in hand. A large piece of wood fell off the workpiece. Hastily squeezing a dab of poly-vinyl acetate on both surfaces, I went on chatting to my attentive audience and let the adhesive get tacky, then I shoved the broken piece into place. The odd thing was that nobody seemed to notice, and less than two hours later I was merrily planing and sawing the piece without any trouble at all.

When two or more pieces of wood are bonded together and have to be included in any construction where they will be visible, you have to disguise the fact. The many techniques which can be used are not within the scope of this book, but you may like to consult my earlier book, *The finishing and re-finishing of wood* (Constable, 1969).

If the wit of craftsmen is proverbially sharp, then it only matches many of the edged tools they use in their work. Sharpness is vitally important. Anybody who is concerned with teaching the young should remember that the sharper the tool, the safer it is. You need only attempt to force a blunt chisel through a piece of wood to know the danger of slips and skids caused by the brute force which has to be used. It is like shaving. Use a blunt blade and you end up with a bloody face. Use a blunt tool and you end up with a multilated finger. I remember a lady, over eighty years old, who once persuaded me to show her how to work with wood. Although my wife and I went to immense pains to show her how to sharpen the tools, she somehow failed to master the technique. A few days later she came to see us again, trying to hide a bandaged wrist. At last she admitted: 'I got so interested in what you said that I was lying in bed and it was going round and round in my head, so I thought I'd just try it out, and it was three o'clock in the morning, so I sat up in my bed with the tools you told me to get and I had a piece of wood handy, and somehow the chisel slipped and went into my vein, so they took me to hospital and gave me a transfusion.' She then produced the chisel. It was as blunt as my backside.

Some people lash out and buy their tools and benches and everything else in sight, but they leave the grindstone till last of all. It's odd, because sharpness of edged tools is vital. A lot depends on your budget. The idea of spending £20, £30 or more on a powered grindstone is daunting enough in comparison with a few shillings for a hand grindstone, but what it boils down is whether you want a labour-saving device or you are content to spend time sweating over a hand stone. In my own experience, there is more to it than that. Put a beginner on a powered stone and he will 'burn' the tool into uselessness within a few minutes, shoving the steel down against the revolving wheel and holding it there until the friction build-up will turn the metal cherry red and then blue. Within a couple of seconds it is slaughtered, because the softening creeps straight up the blade. It should be added that a coolant must be used, and this can be a water drip onto the wheel at the point of contact with the tool. If the flow is right, the tool will not burn. But the best thing you

can do is watch a professional using a powered stone.
He lays it on the stone for only a few seconds at a
time, removing it to look at it closely, because it is
rarely that a perfect bevel can be achieved by simply
laying it against the stone. If the job is done in short
bursts, there is obviously much less danger of friction
building up.

The average bench grinder costs between £21 and
£48. It weighs between 22 lb. and 32 lb. and it is fitted
as a rule with two grinding wheels, either 6 in. or 8 in.,
one coarse and the other fine. It will also be fitted with
transparent shields as a guard against splashback and
the shower of almost microscopic steel fragments
which are thrown off by the wheel when it runs at
about 2950 rpm. Without the shield and using plenty
of coolant, you will develop a broad black streak from
your chest to your *symphysis pubis*. It doesn't do your
shirt any good, either.

There is a temptation to spend less than you should
on a bench grinder, especially when you are faced with
the blandishments of the bargain pages in the
newspapers. Too late, you find that a cheap job suffers
from wheel wobble due to bad spindle fitting. Then
there is the danger of the wheel itself disintegrating.
Some wheels break up without warning, and the effect
is like getting shrapnel in your face. Because these
cheap machines are powered by badly insulated
motors, which are easily affected by moisture seepage,
there is always the chance of electrocuting yourself or
blowing the main fuse. You need only see a grinder in
action and note the way moisture is thrown off to settle

in a fine film on the motor casing to realise what can happen. I once knew a craftswoman who misguidedly bought a cheap grinder and as soon as she started using it she was electrocuted and flung back against the workshop wall.

In the better machines, such as the Wolf No. 4250 and 4218,* the greatest possible expert attention has been paid to isolating the electric motor. It is a very important factor, especially in industrial workshops, where any number of people may be using the same grinder, but also at an amateur level, where there is a tendency to ignore safety factors. To narrow the margin of danger the Wolf designers have done away completely with the earthing lead—but this is something we will talk about in the section on power tools.

It is best to buy a good bench grinder later rather than sooner, and I think that the beginner should get the feel of tools and know how to sharpen them by using a handstone. For instance, the hard Arkansas stone, 5 in. × 2 in. × 1 in. which may cost £4 or £5, will last a lifetime, and it gives just as good an edge as the bench grinder, even if it does take a bit longer. There is a wide variety of stones on the market. Some of them are coarse on one side and fine on the other, and they cost from £1·25 to £1·50. The ordinary India bench stone costs about £1·25.

* Wolf Electric Tools Limited, Pioneer Works, Hanger Lane, London, W. 5.

Stones, which are made from manufactured material or natural stone, quickly clog up. Like the human skin, stones have pores, and when they are full of lubricating oil and fragments of steel they quickly become ineffective. You can tell when this happens because the tool will slide over the surface instead of biting against it. When a stone is in good condition, the tool whispers over it. When the stone is dull, the tool merely rumbles up and down and you get nowhere with it.

It's surprising how many people walk into a shop and buy a stone, and then start using it without any preparation at all except to slop oil over its surface. You can get more out of it if you first of all prime it by soaking thoroughly in a mixture of oil and kerosene (2 parts oil to one of kerosene). This shifts the warehouse muck and frees the microscopic particles of stone against which the tool may bind. I generally let the stone soak in the priming fluid for up to a week and repeat the treatment every few months if the stone is in regular use. If it does get badly clogged up, boil it and then prime it before using. For a quick clean I can recommend lighter fluid and a good rub with a rag. A really sleepy stone can be wakened by boiling it for half-an-hour or so in a dilute solution of soda.

A great deal of learned prattle has been uttered about the right sort of oil to be used on stones. Exotic oils I have never heard of are advocated, columns of print are used to explain the whys and the wherefores. To be blunt about it, the only purpose of the oil is to lubricate and help the tool to move over the surface of the stone. You can use thick or thin oil, a medium cycle oil or, at a pinch, the thinner typewriter oil. A back street trader friend of mine once bought fifty gallons of ordinary cycle oil and he could not get rid of it at any price, so he bought several gross of glass bottles, had labels printed and then unloaded the lot on to the amateur craftsman market. The label said that the oil was 'specially blended' for use on oil stones. Some months later he showed me a file full of testimonials from happy users, all of them the victims of their own imagination.

While you are sharpening the tools on the stone, a kind of feather, or burr, will form on the edge of the tool. It all depends on the angle at which you hold the tool. When you first touch up a factory sharpened tool fresh from the manufacturer, you get an accumulation of swarf, which is the technical name for it. In tools which have been used for some years there will be less swarf. Whichever way it goes, the swarf has to be removed from the edge of the tool before you can use it, and the correct way of doing this is by using what is called a slipstone. They are made in many different shapes, from round to wedge and they will fit practically any shape of tool. Like the stone itself, they should be well lubricated. The best way is by securing the tool in vice or hand and then rubbing the slipstone (one way only) against the feather, or burr, which should fall away after a few strokes. It is advisable to use a steady pressure, but do not try to modify the edge, which has already been imparted by the stone, otherwise you can create variable bevels.

When you sharpen a tool you use an abrasive action. Abrasion is used more than you might think in woodworking. Take sandpaper, for instance. Like other sheeted abrasives it comes in a wide range, from very fine to very coarse, denoted by a series of alphabetical and numerical prefixes in the form of a code, and it is packed—but not necessarily sold—in quantities of a ream (500 sheets) or quire (25 sheets).

Other abrasives include:

Flexible Blue Twill ($00–1\frac{1}{2}$ and 2–3) is among the more expensive, but it is a good investment because it is durable and long lasting if rather stiff to start with.
White Back Emery Cloth ($00–1\frac{1}{2}$ and 2–3) is slightly less expensive and has about two-thirds of the life of flexible blue twill.
Glass Cloth (00–F2, M2 and S2, $2\frac{1}{2}$ and 3) has a fairly long life with many utility applications.
Waterproof Glass Paper ($0–1–1\frac{1}{2}$, F2, M2, S2, $2\frac{1}{2}$) is a common utility paper.

I have always thought that sanding wood is a laborious process, especially if you work through from coarse to very fine, finishing off with pumice powder and felt cut from old hats, although you can achieve a lovely satin appearance. This occupies a lot of time and several pints of sweat, which explains why so many wood finishers in Victorian days died as a result of happy dipsomania, replacing sweat with beer. Nowadays the emphasis is on speed and a superficially good external appearance, so many amateurs prefer to use a power sander which gives a presentable appearance in a fraction of the time it used to take working by hand. It has its drawbacks, too, of course, because if you are not paying attention to what you are doing, you can rub out any fine detail. One of my more eccentric cousins spent many weeks creating an intricate moulding. None of the shop stuff for him! Every inch was handworked. When it was to his liking, he reached for his power sander and joyfully ran it up and down the surface. Because the work was already very delicate, he not only whisked it out of existence but he also managed to reduce the moulding itself to a wafer thinness in a few moments. They say that these new abrasives are very effective. It is quite true. Sometimes they are too effective. It depends on what you decide to use. Here are some notes on abrasives and their qualities:

Aluminium Oxide, which cuts very sharply into the wood when it is under pressure, is particularly useful if you are tackling a surface which is coarse or pitted. I have often used it on mill-sawn Pirana pine and created a perfectly smooth surface in a few minutes.
Garnet Paper, which is widely used in cabinet making, is useful when it comes to the more delicate work. Garnet paper is available in coarse to fine grades, and you can get it in soft papers, which are handy for

working at awkward angles or in narrow corners.

Flint paper, which you will use in large quantities, and you often find yourself rubbing your fingertips into the wood if you are not using a block.

In the last few years some firms have attempted to produce wood, metal and plastic blocks around which the abrasive sheet can be wrapped and clipped into position. These blocks have their uses, of course, but I always use cork—a small round cork fishing net float which I found on the tide line of the Bristol Channel is still going strong after seven or eight years' use. Failing cork, you can always use various sizes of wood block, but when it comes to detailed and intricate work, I prefer to use my own hand as a block, curling the sandpaper round my finger.

I am not suggesting that you should keep several reams of assorted abrasives in the workbench drawer. Half-a-dozen sheets of the finest, the 'middles' and the coarse will always be useful. It should be kept dry, otherwise it will tear if it is even slightly moist. If you are faking antiques for a living, different grades of pumice powder should be kept stored in glass jars. For general utility purposes the medium/fine no. 2/0 is probably the best. After buying it, you should spread it out on a sheet of newspaper and sort out any coarse granules which may have crept through the manufacturer's sieve, otherwise you will find that it scratches the wood.

Here is a handy comparison table of abrasives to suggest similarities between the different types.

Glasspaper	Garnet	Aluminium Oxide	Flint Paper	Emery Cloth
—	10/0	10/0	10/0	—
—	9/0	9/0	9/0	—
—	8/0	8/0	8/0	—
—	7/0	7/0	7/0	—
—	6/0	6/0	6/0	—
00	5/0	5/0	5/0	0
0	4/0	4/0	4/0	FF
1	3/0	3/0	3/0	F
$1\frac{1}{2}$	2/0	2/0	2/0	1
F2	0	0	0	$1\frac{1}{2}$
M2	$\frac{1}{2}$	$\frac{1}{2}$	$\frac{1}{2}$	2
—	—	—	—	$2\frac{1}{2}$
S2	1	1	1	3
$2\frac{1}{2}$	$1\frac{1}{2}$	$1\frac{1}{2}$	$1\frac{1}{2}$	4
3	2	2	2	—

You can also use steel wool for smooth wood. Six grades are available, as follows:

Grade no.	Uses
3	Very coarse and useful for rubbing down rough surfaces
2	Cuts rapidly on fairly rough wood
1	For general utility, and especially good for preparing panels for sanding
0	A utility grade for hard and soft woods
00	General use
000	For final smoothing

2 Chisels

As a general rule, chisels are used for forcing screws into wood, stirring paint, levering up can lids and also for inflicting ugly wounds on yourself or other people. Although they are specialist tools, we often use them for many other things—that's if we are stupid enough to do so, of course. They are just dumb tools, they do not protest.

The chisel is much abused and little respected, because it is not generally realised that it is a comparatively limited tool, designed for a specific use which we will go into later. You can pay a high price for a good chisel or else you can make one, which is done by grinding down a file on an electric grinding wheel. This is a long process and you generally get coated in fine steel particles, even when the wheel is shielded. The home-made chisel, which is used for carving or for general utility purposes, is your mate for life, and those of us who are sufficiently old-fashioned to actually like making our own tools tend to form a small clique, like the collectors of rare gems. The trouble with most commercial chisels is that they are made in a certain range of sizes, and so they sometimes do not suit the pernickety craftsman because they are either too long or too short, or otherwise inadequate for the job in hand. It has always seemed to me that there is great scope for some small firm which could make tools to a customer's own specification. None of us mind paying a little extra for something special. In fact, one fellow I know who wanted an exceptionally long chisel for a job worth £150 to him had it done by a back-street firm, and it cost £7, although it was used but once for that particular job. It is only during the last half century or so that chisels have been made in a standard range. Before that it was the custom to give the task to the senior apprentice in charge of tool making, and steel was shaped, heated and hammered, and the edge finally put on by the man who started out with the length of metal while a junior apprentice cranked the great grinding wheel. Many of these tools are still in regular use. I have a one-inch chisel forged in some small workshop in Scotland, and while the shaft is noticeably thicker than in the modern counterpart, it takes an edge which can last for months of hard work. Now that I have converted it into a double-bevelled tool, it is used for woodcarving, because it is superb for removing large quantities of wood in a short time.

Long before apprentices were toolmakers, the craftsman was making his own implements. I used to live in South Wales, where some of the most impressive archaeological finds of Bronze Age chisels occurred. They are now lodged at the National Museum of Wales and are in a fine state of preservation, probably due to the nature of the soil in

which they were found, at a depth of only three feet.
They look as though you could pick them up and use
them. The Bronze Age craftsman evidently believed in
making a lasting job of it, because the remains of these
tools have rivet holes rather than the collar or modern
tang. The tang itself has a lengthy heritage, and it
seems to have been introduced in Scandinavia about
one thousand years ago. Although it is not necessarily
the best way of marrying the tool to the handle, it is
nowadays used extensively, probably because it is the
most economical method of production. If a flange
with rivet holes were used, this would mean extra
manufacturing operations. During the Iron Age,
from which relatively few specimens have come down
to us, a different method of fixing was used, embodying
a kind of flange, or lip. The closest equivalent to the
modern chisel was born in Roman times and it had a
very long handle. The question of handles has been
debated by generations of craftsmen, and while it may
seem unimportant to the layman, it is a fact that the
longer-than-usual tool can work wonders in manipulation and effectiveness. For instance, I often use a
gouge which is six inches long and has a handle of
equal length. This makes a total of one foot. The
feeling you get when you are using it is one of total
freedom, especially when working at awkward angles.

When you use tools, a bit of skill is always a necessary ingredient. Knocking a nail into a piece of wood
demands balanced judgement and just the right
amount of force, otherwise the nail will bend. To a

layman, laying a piece of steel on a grinding wheel to put a cutting edge on it looks easy. But it isn't. For one thing, unless the steel is at the proper angle to the wheel, the result will be uneven grinding and the appearance of many little facets as the grip wavers. Glass cutting provides another example. I never cease to marvel at the way the craftsman casually cuts plate glass, using a tool which is almost invisible in his clenched fist. It is an art which I have never mastered, and my own attempts have to be made with vast reserves of glass available. There isn't a craftsman who does not have his own particular methods—the so-called trade secrets—and chisel-making has always been in this department, especially as far as the bevel, or angle, is concerned. Between the tenth and thirteenth centuries the Russian tool-makers used an angle of 25 degrees on the bevel with a much narrower blade than the modern chisel. Here again, the question of length comes in, because during the same period the European tool-makers were producing much shorter chisels with a kind of fish-tailed blade. Of the two different types, the narrow Russian tool was probably the best, because anything fish-tailed has an uncanny habit of sliding off course unless a great deal of strength and control is used.

The family tree of the chisel varies, because over a period of thousands of years it has been used in different forms in many trades. Some have died as the trades themselves have died—and what is sadder than the death of a trade? Many thousands of coopers have

gone out of business in the last few years, because
metal casks are being used for beer and other liquids,
although I am told that the whisky distillers still
employ Scottish and Irish coopers. I remember the late
Edric Connor, singer and actor, describing to me his
early days as an apprentice in a London cooperage.
Although he was talking about events of less than
thirty years before, the trade was dying even then. I
suppose this is something we have to face. By the time
total industrial automation becomes a fact, the
museums will be full of factory machinery and tools.
Industry produces its own dodos with incredible
rapidity. So it is not impossible that by the year 2000
AD we will be peering at today's wood chisels resting
in museum cases.

At the present time such manual trades as are still
left use between them about thirty or forty different
kinds of chisels, but in terms of ordinary
woodworking, the following are considered quite
sufficient for most jobs, from building small bookcases
to kitchen cabinets or, say, the preparation of roof
battens and constructional joinery:

Firmer chisels
Bevel edge firmer
   chisels
Long thin paring
   chisels

All available
in the following sizes:
$\frac{3}{16}$; $\frac{1}{4}$; $\frac{1}{2}$; $\frac{5}{8}$; $\frac{3}{4}$; $\frac{7}{8}$; 1; $1\frac{1}{8}$; $1\frac{1}{4}$;
$1\frac{3}{4}$; 2 inches.

Woodworking Tools

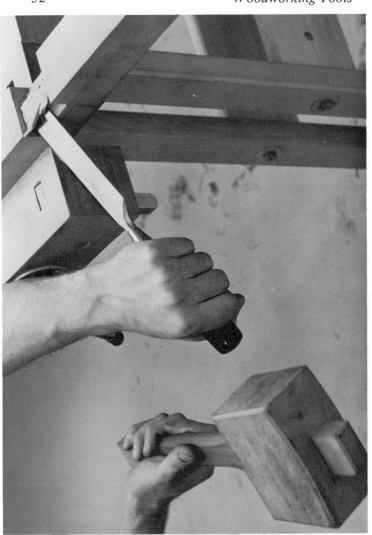

Wrap the fist round the chisel handle when using the mallet

The correct way to hold a wood chisel

I know that many experts suggest that the beginner should start off with only four chisels ($\frac{1}{4}$ in; $\frac{1}{2}$ in; $\frac{3}{4}$ in. and 1 in.), but this seems to be a typical case of spoiling the ship for the usual ha'porth of tar. It is much better to buy a selection to begin with rather than going to a shop and buying one of those smartly presented sets in transparent cases. As far as the handles are concerned, I am not sure why so many manufacturers are now favouring the hard plastic ones, because anybody in his right mind prefers ash or boxwood. A manufacturer told me about the ease with which these moulded plastic handles can be produced and fitted, using unskilled labour, and he was quite surprised when I told him how difficult they can be under working conditions. They had, he protested, 'field and laboratory tested' the plastic handles. They had even put them under giant presses to test them for strength; they had just rigged up a machine to see how many million blows these handles could withstand. The one thing they overlooked was the fact that a wet plastic handle is harder to hold than a wooden one. He admitted that they had never actually wetted the handles and then tested them. I suggested that he sit up on the roof of a half-finished house in a high wind with the rain or sleet coming down, and then try and use tools with plastic handles. But here, as in so many other things nowadays, it seems to be more important to produce the goods in vast quantities instead of ensuring that they are what the craftsman needs. There is such a lack of choice that some manufacturers are sure of a profitable market. Future generations will not even realise that these tools once had wooden handles which, after a year or two of use, produced a very useful blob at the top, making a kind of cushion for the mallet or hammer. Plastic handles are resilient and they may even outlast the user, but ash or boxwood are also tough. If you do come across some wooden handles and you want to fit them to tools, the first thing to do is heat the tang to a cherry red with a blowtorch and then sink it into the handle. I notice that chisels and handles are still sold separately by little old men in independent toolshops.

For devotees of the age of the plastic prepack, however, a set of firmer bevel edge chisels in the most popular sizes can be bought for about £3·50 (four chisels), £4 (5 chisels) or £5 (six chisels). Some manufacturers now prepack these selections in blister packs, which precludes the possibility of inspecting the goods before buying them, and they seem to have overlooked the fact that tool buyers, like buyers of books, prefer to finger the merchandise before forking out. While we are about it, let us just mention the fact that the manufacturers seem to be very fond of standardising handle and tool lengths. As we already know, length of handle does exert a definite influence not only on the user but also the job itself, and this is particularly applicable in the case of chisels when short and narrow mortices have to be cut. For this reason it is advisable to buy your first selection of chisels one by one, including butt chisels with a blade no more than $3\frac{1}{4}$ inches long, followed by the more popular lengths.

As I said earlier, the role of the chisel is not a versatile one. For instance, you would not attempt to trim the end of a board with a chisel, no matter how sharp it happened to be, because it is unlikely that it would do it satisfactorily. This applies especially to soft woods like pine, which have a nasty habit of chipping or splintering. It is far better to use a small plane for these tasks. Where there is a tolerance of up to about $\frac{1}{2}$ inch I always use a bandsaw, especially if undertaking a job like facing walls with knotty pine in tongue and groove jointing. If a chisel is used, the ends will probably chip, marring the final appearance.

So what is the true role of the chisel? As I have already said, it is not versatile and it cannot be used for everything. The major role is in making narrow recesses for joints, cutting recesses to accommodate butt hinges and the like. Whatever the job, the first rule for working with a sharp chisel is to use gentleness and persuasion. Nothing is more infuriating than to mark out and score the area of a joint only to accidentally chop out far more than was intended by a ham-fisted shove or hammer clout.

If a very sharp chisel is to be treated with the utmost caution, a blunt chisel should be treated with disdain. Trying to use a poorly sharpened chisel is like trying to paint with a de-bristled brush. I am often asked about children and sharp tools, and when I tell parents that it is a mistake to let youngsters start out with blunt tools, they think I am mad. To them a blunt tool seems so much safer. But just imagine trying to make a cut with a blunt chisel! You push and you shove, and you put all your weight behind it and it suddenly jerks and slips, and you cut your hand or arm. Now, imagine a razor-edged tool which whispers smoothly and sweetly through the wood at the slightest pressure. You have confidence in it because it goes where it is sent. A child will recognize this at once and there is no reason why anything should go wrong once a basic rule has been drummed into the small head. That rule is: always have both hands *behind* the tool. Many children and even adults have a tendency to 'cuddle' their way round the job and so the arm which is not holding the tool snakes round until it is directly in the path of the chisel. If the field of work is well illuminated, and the job is firmly clamped in position to the bench with G-cramps or bench stops, and providing the bench is the correct height, there is no danger from a chisel. But even when an accident does happen, if the tool is razor sharp, it will cut very cleanly and there will not be half as much pain as you get with a blunted tool and the edges of the cut should knit together without trouble. Blunt tools cause ugly scars, sharp ones don't. Basically, it is a mistake to keep children away from sharp tools, although I must admit to some anxious moments when Ruth, my daughter, has taken it into her head to sort out the contents of my tool box. Restrictions will only result in curious small hands raiding the chest in secret, and the illicit experiment may well end in bloodshed.

A chisel should never be left unsharpened, even
when it is not in use for considerable periods, and the
habit of keeping an edge on it should be as much a
part of the process as using it. When it leaves the
factory it will have an edge of a sort, but it is by no
means suitable for working. It is simply a starting
point on which you must form the 25–30 degree bevel.
This is not necessarily the most desirable working
bevel for general purposes, because an angle of 30 to
35 degrees is just as good. I do not pretend that it is
easy to get a perfect bevel. It isn't. It can be the most
frustrating job, and it is not surprising that many
beginners cart their chisels round the tool shops,
looking for somebody to do it for them. Yet to my
mind it is like buying a pair of boots and a set of laces
and then asking somebody else to do your walking for
you. If you practice sharpening a pencil with a sharp
knife and cutting the wood evenly all round it will help
to train your eyes. I don't favour the powered bench
grinder for chisel sharpening, because it is fatally easy
to ruin the tool. Far better to use a gauge on a nice
even stone, or even do without a gauge, because
although it might take longer to get the right bevel,
you do get the 'feel' of the tool. Hand sharpening needs
plenty of oil so that the detached particles of steel are
floated off. Lack of oil clogs up the stone.

The real art of imparting a bevel is in holding the
tool at the correct angle without any deviation or
rocking. After a quarter of an hour of muscular push-

ing and pulling, it is fatally easy to drift off into the rocking motion which will round off the corners of the chisel. It can also cause the small facets to appear. As you correct one, another appears, and so you go on until nothing short of professional regrinding will put the fault right. If you are a beginner you can quickly learn the rights and the wrongs of angles by placing a small reading lamp at one end of the stone and then looking along the length of the stone as the tool is held in position on it. The light will show any hollows in the edge itself and any small edge chips.

The amount of pressure to be used when sharpening is governed by the strength of the user. It is no good simply stroking the tool against the stone, because nothing will happen. A really forceful and calculated push downwards will make the steel bite against the stone, setting up a particular kind of hissing sound, which means that the metal is being worn down. If a gauge is used, this sound will not be so noticeable, because the action is semi-mechanised. The gauge has one great virtue insofar as the angle can be pre-set and the tool clamped in position. By moving the tool in the gauge, the angle can be varied. The gauge itself is cheap enough, less than £1·25, and it consists quite simply of a thumbscrew and a swivel pad, like a castor, which runs up and down the stone.

A well-sharpened chisel is a very delicate tool, and so it pays to store it carefully. In the workshop it can rest in a wall rack with the edges well protected. If it has to be carried about, then a felt roll is a good idea with one side sewn up to hold the sharp edges firm. A double precaution consists of lining the separate compartments of the tool roll with oiled felt to resist rust and corrosion.

3   Hammers

You might think that of all tools the hammer must have been with us from the earliest times, when it was probably just a crudely shaped piece of metal stuck on the end of a handle, or shaft, and it has come down to us by a process of evolution so that it has ended up as a scientifically balanced tool with an assortment of differently shaped heads for specific purposes. This is not so! The hammer has a peculiar history and a very patchy one, and it did not by any means start its life in the way I have suggested. Technological history is not always easy to chart or trace, because development tends to waver; it is affected by factors like the ingenuity of the artisan, who introduced his own modifications, or a brainwave of somebody in the research and development department of a firm. I remember running a value analysis seminar for a firm which employed the best brains in the country, and one of the problems tossed into their laps was to devise twelve uses for a common hammer. They could not think of one—not even as a prop for an open window.

A friend of mine with a physics degree spent more than a year designing a better hammer, including the handle, and creating a new tapered head with a larger contact surface, the main idea being that it would carry greater force but use up less energy on the part of the operator. It was a very unusual looking hammer, a real symbol of the future, and it was so beautifully made that it should have been in a glass case. We tested it in the drawing office where he worked. It cost him over £30 for a new window after it flew out of his hand, thereby demonstrating that it did possess rather more built-in energy than the conventional version. Work on the new model was discontinued. Even so, there is still some scope for research into the dynamics of the hammer, although it will take a brave man—or woman—to undertake it.

The hammer probably evolved indirectly from the Egyptian mallet, which was nothing more or less than a chunk of wood on a stick. On the other hand, the whole tool might have been carved out of a single piece of wood with the striking part shaped and balanced for accuracy. It is impossible to tell how long all this took in terms of time, because the great dynasties of Egypt went on for thousands of years and mallets may well have become hammers during this period, their design affected by such diverse trades as shipbuilding and house, palace and tomb construction.

Once out of the Egyptian period and into medieval times, a more recognisable pattern emerged, and the hammer appeared with interchangeable heads, some of them with dual purposes, such as the adze and the hammer itself. It is significant that dual-purpose tools have never really given much satisfaction to the user. From what we do know about the medieval craftsman, he hated his hammer-cum-adze or what-have-you. The same applies to today's multi-purpose tools, although the persistent manufacturers still go on launching their gimmicks every year. As far as the hammer is concerned, opportunities for duality are very limited, disregarding the combined claw and ball pein. Some years ago I was amused to see what the manufacturer claimed to be what he called a 'revolution' in hammers, consisting of a set of heads for various purposes and a standard shaft. It was, he said, much more up to date than nuclear power. Had the copywriters given a bit more thought to it, they would have done their homework more thoroughly and found out that the selfsame principle was used by Iron Age man and, at a later date, by other civilisations, who used leather or cord thongs to firmly secure the different heads. Even the claw hammer is ancient, because in the Iron Age the toolmaker was forging hammer heads with holes bored through them for lifting out iron staples.

A new phase of hammer development occurred in Britain during the Industrial Revolution. Although the individual shapes varied very little, individual names were used. Having examined a large number of them in museums, I am inclined to believe that these names were used for commercial purposes, because all the heads are practically identical. The heads were probably mass produced and sold, and the handles were fitted by the tool factor, who was the forerunner of the modern ironmonger. At that time the

'Dorchester' hammer was sold only in the town of that name, the 'Wigan', the 'London' and other patterns likewise, and, if the craftsman's diaries of that period are to be believed, the ruse was so convincing that industrial workers absolutely swore by their local hammer, believing it to be absolutely unique and superior to all other hammers. Although it may seem that hammers have in the last fifty years become fewer and more standardised, I see that the catalogue of a national tool dealer offers no less than 66 varieties, from the adze eye to the famous Warrington, which is perhaps the standardised descendant of all those local specialities. The Warrington is still the most popular hammer in modern use.

There are two characteristics which are shared by all hammers, the curved claw and the straight claw, and they are incorporated in nailing hammers. Together with the straight-faced hammer and the ball pein, they are adequate enough for most types of work. A well-made hammer consists of head and handle. It is as simple as that. But there are both inferior and superior specimens. A cheap hammer will have a couple of nails or staples driven into the head, expanding the wood against the inside of the collar. This is totally inadequate and can result in serious accidents. The well-made hammer has two metal wedges and a wooden one, which are driven in so tightly that it will be quite impossible to pull the head off the handle, and there will be no rocking or 'give'. In fact, it is said that a pull of more than four tons is

Standard Warrington hammer

needed to separate head from handle. Even so, the
worst enemies of the hammer can be excessive dryness
or excessive moisture. Either of these can loosen the
hammer head, although some of the makers are now
using synthetic resins to bond one to the other.

If you want the kind of hammer which can be left
lying about in boiler rooms or on damp building
sites, there is the steel-handled model. Some of these
are made in one piece, others incorporate a special
locking device which makes the head immovable.
Both types are fitted with different kinds of easy-grip
handles, some of them moulded to suit the grip of the
fingers and palm, others fluted, and this moulding also
acts as a shock absorber. Although the all-metal
hammers look 'with-it' and suggest extra efficiency,
some of the lighter, cheaper ones do not contain
enough weight to develop a good contact force, so they
call for more muscular power, which can be tiring.

Some time ago an importer of steel hammers and
other tools presented me with one and urged me to
give it what he called 'a good bashing'. During the next
couple of weeks I did just that, ignoring the slowly
buckling handle. When it finally snapped, I found that
it was hollow, so I sent back the pices with a polite
note. He protested that I had given his prize import too
much of a bashing. I retaliated by saying that any
hammer ought to be able to deliver an average of 45
foot-pounds with a contact pressure of more than half
a ton per square inch, and levering a nail out with a
claw hammer should produce as much as 1,000 lbs

All-steel hammer, useful for outdoor work in wet weather

at the point between handle and head, given a handle
between twelve and fifteen inches long. It all goes
to show that you must not go solely by appear-
ances, especially where all-metal tools are concerned. Poor quality metal will eventually become
fatigued, it will crack, split or shatter, and so the
difficulty of choosing a quality hammer with up to half
a century of life in it is that one metal looks very much
like another. Nothing short of analysis will give you
an opinion about the quality of the materials used.

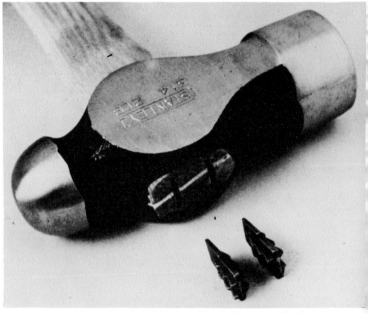

Two steel wedges hold the head of the hammer firmly in
place

Properly used, the claw hammer produces up to 1000
lbs pressure when extracting a nail

Apart from the worth of wood and metal, there is also the question of the design and the manufacture of the tool itself. The handle will be rounded and set straight; the steel wedges will hold the head firm; the grain of the wood will run parallel to the head. If the head has been painted to disguise this, do not buy at any price. Particular attention should be paid to the planes of the head, especially on the striking surface. There used to be a trick played on simple apprentices, who were given a hammer with a slightly distorted handle and a striking surface which had been ground down to create a tilt. The tool was known as the 'fool's hammer' and it was virtually impossible to drive a nail in straight and true.

A lot can be said about the right weight for a hammer. It is not just a matter of buying the heaviest under the impression that it will do for all jobs. For instance, if you work in the confined space of an attic, replacing or securing joists and lying on your belly most of the time, a 16 oz. hammer soon begins to weigh a ton. On the other hand, a hammer of lighter weight will lessen fatigue, although more force will be needed to drive long nails well and truly home. Again, a cabinet maker would not use a 16 oz. hammer. He would prefer the 11 oz. model. It is all a matter of personal preference, and it can be illustrated by trying out various weights, holding the hammers by the end of the handle and swinging them. Ergonomically speaking, this is the right way of using a hammer, keeping both wrist and forearm rigid. If you use only a wrist action, it will result in less striking power and fatigue. I was once testing hammers in a tool shop to the bewilderment of the young girl assistant, who kept producing them from box after box. Presently, she found a 20 oz. claw hammer—a grand looking specimen costing £1·50. She then came round to my side of the counter to watch my performance. Standing just a little too close, I caught the sharp claw in her overall and ripped it from top to bottom.

And the best hammers for the beginner? Well, I would recommend one curved claw of 28 oz., a ripping hammer of 16 oz., a Warrington of 16 oz., and, for lighter work, the $3\frac{1}{2}$ oz. cross pein and the pin, or telephone, 4 oz. hammer.

There is not a great deal to be said about the care and maintenance of hammers beyond the fact that the handles should be kept smoothed, and oiled now and then with linseed oil to preserve them. The striking part of the metal head must be kept free of grease and corrosion. Some craftsmen polish the heads with emery cloth, but I do not recommend this, because the shine and the glitter can be very distracting, especially when you are working outside in bright sunshine. As far as claw hammers are concerned, the jaws should be kept sharp and the V-shape well pronounced to make sure that the tool can be forced down to get a purchase on even the smallest nail head.

4 Screwdrivers

That whiskery old joke about the left-handed screwdriver is not a joke at all. It is a fact that a right-angled screwdriver—known as a 'round-the-corner' screwdriver—can be bought for about 25 p. It is a useful tool for driving in screws when they are located in awkward corners. Another use is for driving in screws on the undersides of shelves, also coffins which are too heavy to turn on the trestles.

The screwdriver is a youngster. It has no particular history in the sense that saws and hammers and other tools have an ancestry which can be traced. But, as in other areas of tool design, it has been mercilessly adapted so that today we have ratchet drivers and drivers with oddly shaped handles, some of them up to eighteen inches long, and other neat little things which fit into the palm of the hand. There are fat ones and thin ones. There are those which inflict a blister on the palm because they have badly milled ends.

The characteristics of a good screwdriver should consist of (a) a handle which can be gripped—and I do mean gripped; (b) a blade of sufficient tensile strength to tackle the job for which it is intended; (c) a blade length which is not too long and not too short so that pressure causes wavering. Of course, finding a tool which measures up to all these requirements is quite another matter. Probably the best is the commonest, namely the cabinet screwdriver with a 'London' type bulbous and tapered handle made of beech with a brass ferrule and a plain steel blade in sizes from 2 in. to 12 in. For greater strength there is always the half-brother of the cabinet, rather smugly known in the trade as the 'perfect handle' with a solid cast steel blade running the whole length of the handle and riveted hardwood inserts to form the handle.

It is hardly necessary to list the variations of this standard screwdriver except to mention the ratchet model, which sometimes has a habit of slipping its gears at crucial moments, causing the blade to jerk and, in all probability, gouge into the surrounding wood. The fact that some manufacturers and distributors have maintenance departments to restore sick ratchets speaks for itself. They can go wrong and they do go wrong. My own opinion is that it is probably more economical to buy one each of the London type screwdriver rather than spend as much as £2 on a poor quality ratchet model. Another drawback to the ratchet is that the pumping action does create a tendency to push the screw home somewhat too rapidly and this can be very dangerous when you are doing delicate work. You would not, for instance, use a ratchet screwdriver for cabinet work (in any case, it is better to use dowels instead of screws for cabinet making), although it might be suitable for fixing door hinges or window frames and other coarse joinery of that kind. As far as the business of driving a screw home properly and accurately is concerned, the non-ratchet screwdriver beats its more modern counterpart hands down. It might take longer, it might not be in accord with modern methods, but it is at least sure. Whereas the ratchet will push the screw in at the wrong angle before a correction can be made, the old type pushes it straight in thread by thread. A lot more sweat, I quite agree, but a lot more satisfaction, too.

Some people think that one screwdriver will do absolutely everything, but the well-equipped toolchest will have no less than five. Here are the sizes with the equivalent screw sizes:

$\frac{1}{4}$ in.	6–8
$\frac{5}{16}$ in.	8–12
$\frac{1}{8}$ in.	12–16
$\frac{7}{16}$ in.	16–20
$\frac{1}{2}$ in.	20–24

All five screwdrivers should have blades of the standard keystone shape.

Then there are the variations on the screwdriver. For instance, there is the offset screwdriver with a 5 in. lever to provide increased power, and it is useful for shifting recalcitrant screws. There is another type of screwdriver fitted with jaws to clamp the screw more tightly and hold it in position until the blade engages the slot and makes a few turns, after which the jaws can be retracted. It is very useful for inserting screws above head height when the surface cannot be reached by ladder.

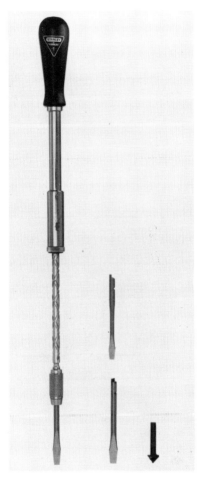

Ratchet screwdriver with interchangeable bits and countersink bit

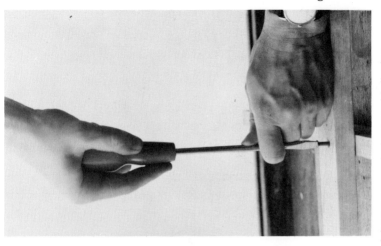

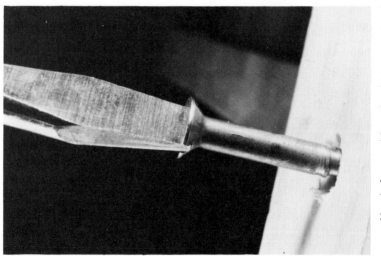

Head of screwdriver should engage the slot of the screw precisely to avoid slipping

Screws

A lot of beginners try to drive a screw into the wood without first of all giving it a start by making a hole with an awl. The hole should not be done to the fullest length of the screw but just deep enough to hold the screw when the driver is applied. The choosing of a screw suitable for any particular job is not unlike the dithering of a woman selecting a new hat. The choice is infinite. Apart from the screws themselves, the range of modern finishes presents a wide selection, from black japanned heads to the anodised finishes. The materials from which the screws are made come in a great variety, too, including aluminium. Old fashioned iron screws are the most durable, but for real aesthetic pleasure you just cannot beat the best brass screws, polished to the richness of gold. I once found a sea-man's chest in a Liverpool junk shop which I should have bought but didn't because I did not have any money on me. I have always regretted it, because it was studded with between eight and ten thousand brass screws—a real museum piece.

Screws are classified by gauge, and the gauge numbers refer to the shank itself, not to the threaded section. Bright mild steel wood screw gauges run from 00 up to 32, with a few omissions, the equivalent sizes being from $\frac{1}{8}$ in. to $1\frac{1}{4}$ in. Brass wood screws, round-headed, are from 00 to 24 gauge and the lengths are from $\frac{1}{8}$ in. to 4 in. The pointed brass wood screw, countersunk head, runs from 00 to 33, the sizes being from $\frac{1}{8}$ in. to $1\frac{1}{2}$ in. or, in another range, from $1\frac{3}{4}$ in. to 6 in.

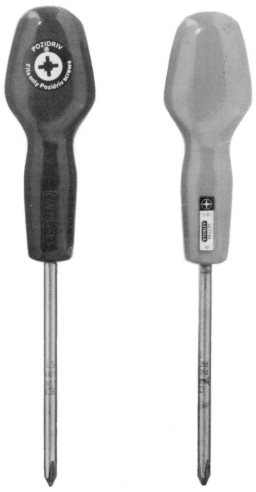

Patent Pozidrive screwdriver with multiple grip action
for use with Pozidrive screws

One tip: depending on the hardness of the wood, it can be exhausting work driving a screw well and truly home. The labour can be reduced by dipping the threaded part of the screw in Vaseline or oil before inserting it in the hole made beforehand by the awl. And, for the sake of posterity, the screw will still be quite easy to remove from between ten and one hundred years hence.

Yet another tip. If countersunk screws are often used, it is worth grinding down the pointed corners of the screwdriver to avoid damaging the wood when the head moves below the surface. But it is best to use the countersink bit before settling in the screw.

5   Planes

The plane is king of the toolchest, because it is one of the oldest of all woodworking implements and can nowadays perform many variations of the basic job which, to the untutored eye, are little short of conjuring tricks. If you want to form a ridge in a piece of planking and then cut a groove to snuggly fit the ridge, this can be done by using a single plane with interchangeable blades. On the other hand if you want to plane in a circle or cut a perfect curve, or flute the edge of a window-pane; if you want to cut a slot into which the glass will slide for glazing, a plane will do the job for you. And, of course, you can use it to plane a true edge on a piece of wood.

There are nearly forty different kinds of planes, from the 3 in. type used by the violin maker up to the 17 in. × $2\frac{1}{2}$ in. jack plane made from steamed English beech. There are the all-metal plough planes with 23 separate cutters which will do practically everything except give you a short back and sides. Setting up the plough plane is a bit like programming a computer, but the perfection of the finished job makes it all worthwhile. It costs up to £10.

Planes in general range from £1 to £25. They are made to high standards, and most of those now on the

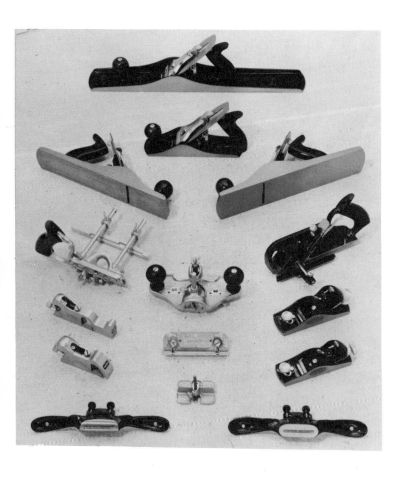

The family of planes

market are completely reliable, including the comparatively recent models, which have disposable blades, doing away with the chore of sharpening (like the Paramo No. 10, which has overcome many difficulties for me in my own work to my complete satisfaction). However, plane blades, or irons as they are called, are very easily sharpened, using a gauge to obtain a constant angle, or bevel. Irons are made from cast steel and they will stand a lot of hard wear providing they do not get into arguments with hidden nails, when they will probably chip.

Although the standard of plane manufacture is high, it is a good idea when you buy one to borrow a steel rule from the man behind the counter and then, with the plane iron fully retracted, place the rule along the bottom of the plane, both straight and diagonally. In so doing, hold the plane up to the light and if the body of the tool is distorted, light will show through. This basic test may aggravate the kind of shopkeeper who is more interested in sheer merchandising than in selling quality goods, but if he does object, you can be sure you are in the wrong shop. If he puts up with your first test, remove the iron from the plane and test the cutting edge for trueness, again using the steel rule. Watch out for slightly bowed plane irons. They will never give a perfectly straight cut.

Nobody has yet discovered when the first plane was used, but back in the 1940s, when I was in Cairo, I visited the Antiquities Museum, which contains some of the spoils from the Valley of the

Kings found by Howard Carter in the thirties. They included a number of murals, as bright in their red and gold as the day they were painted and no doubt preserved by the completely still air of the tomb. I was looking closely at them when I found a section devoted to tradesmen in their various occupations. In the centre was a man using a plane, which looked rather like the modern spokeshave. The date of the mural was approximately 2,500 BC and so 'modern' was the design that I was convinced that no real progress had occurred since that date. Opinions differ about the Egyptian carpenter, and some antiquarians seem to put him down as a user of tools rather than an innovator.

When Pompeii was in the early stages of excavation, a number of petrified planes were found in the solidified ash. Since then, literally hundreds of different kinds of plane have been unearthed at sites throughout the world, so that today we have a comprehensive picture of the history of this particular tool and its different applications. Historians and archaeologists are still trying to decide whether the distribution has any particular significance. For instance, why should the Roman plane have been narrower than the others? And why should the Vikings have created a plane for tongue-and-groove cutting?

You could compile literally hundreds of questions like these, but the answers are simple enough, because planes have always been made to meet the needs of different trades. For instance, the great ocean-going vessels of the Vikings were built on the tongue-and-groove principle, whereas other maritime nations used caulking between close-fitting planking. The Romans adapted their planes for the construction of dwellings and fortifications and the superstructures of earthworks. So all in all, there is really no great mystery about the modification of the plane, which has happened over periods of thousands of years.

One of the best examples of the Roman plane, known as the Caerwent plane, is at Newport Museum, Monmouthshire. There is a minor mystery about this particular model which has worried tool fanciers and archaeologists for many years. The fact is, the sharpening bevel is the wrong way round. The plane could not have been used with it in this position. At first it was assumed to be a weird Roman joke, but the controversy died down and the mystery remained. It does not seem to have occurred to anybody that the plane may have received some rough treatment in its travel down the centuries, and the bevel was, at some stage twisted and never straightened. When corrosion set in, it formed a thick crusty coating so that it is now impossible to find out whether the bevel was accidently twisted or not.

You could write a book on the history of tools, but this one is supposed to be a practical guide. However, I would just like to mention the sixteenth or seventeenth century toolchest in the Victoria and Albert Museum, London, with its treasure trove of finely made tools, many of which have hand-carved carcases. The chest itself looks nondescript outside, but within is inlaid with exquisite marquetry. By practically breaking your neck, it is just possible to catch a glimpse of the richly carved body of a large plane. When the owner of this chest was at work, it is possible that Grinling Gibbons, the emperor of wood carvers, was creating the thick floriation and the cherubim for Blenheim Palace. Perhaps one day, before I am laid in my own box, the Victoria and Albert will find a large showcase and lay those tools out so that we can see them properly, for they are amongst the finest examples of the golden age of English craftsmanship, when craftsmen decorated their tools and housed them in the handsome chests which they designed and made. Many of these chests suggest cabinet maker apprenticeships, for they are akin in style to the designs of Chippendale, when the great English furniture maker and his twenty assistants produced pieces for the nobility in the workshop at St Martin's Lane, London.

The Continental equivalents of these English decorated planes are well worth examining. I can recommend the seventeenth and eighteenth century jointer planes to be seen at the Tiroler Volkskunstmuseum at Innsbruck, Austria, the sixteenth and seventeenth century specimens at the Cleveland Museum of Art, USA, and the miscellaneous lot of eighteenth century smoothing planes at Haslemere Educational Museum, England. I always feel a little sad on seeing tools in glass show cases, because they were intended to be handled and used.

The planes of a century or two ago can still be used and they are just as accurate as today's models. Of course, when you come to think about it, there is very little that can go wrong with a plane apart from a twisted body or a badly sharpened iron. Although this is a very simple tool, it can take quite a bit of practice before you get the hang of planing with the arms and, at the same time, putting all the strength of the shoulder muscles into the action. The other little bit of professionalism which is put into planing is the 'lift' at the end of the stroke so that the tool ascends at exactly the right moment and does not simply fall off the end of the wood, catching you unawares and off balance so that you nosedive straight into the top of the bench. Once you have seen a craftsman at work and noted the even rhythm of planing, you should be able to copy him with some practice. But it is no use looking for this kind of expertise amongst the joiners and carpenters on a building site, because most of the wooden fittings are nowadays prefabricated, very little being made on the site. The best place to see planing done as it should be done is in the workshops of a shopfitting firm, where precision jobs are carried out.

Don't underestimate the amount of energy needed to propel a plane in a perfectly straight line with the right hand clamped over the rear end or, in modern planes, over the contoured handle, and the left one curled over the fore part. The grip must be firm but not absolutely rigid and immovable. Rather than pulling the plane, it should be moved by a pushing action and guided at the same time, the two hands working in harmony and in conjunction with the arm and shoulder muscles. This is much easier to demonstrate than write about. It is like teaching somebody how to play tennis, because a lot must depend on the stance of the body, which should be sideways to the work to allow for a comfortable swing of the trunk. There are many little hints which become self-evident once you start planing, and I would advise the absolutely raw beginner to reduce a narrow plank of pine to shavings, purely for the sake of the practice it gives. You should, of course, start planing at the end of the plank, not in the middle, because while the shavings will be wafer-thin as they curl out of the plane, each one represents a fraction of an inch, and so it is dangerously easy to plane in an irregular curve or create a hollow. If you are making shelves or furniture, it can cause a badly fitting edge. In any case, if you do want to plane in a curve or a hollow, the best tool is either the curved Surform or a spokeshave. I have also done it with a drawknife, but this calls for finesse and expertise. If you are planing a wide, flat piece of wood, adjust the blade so that it takes off rather less than usual, even down to the point where the shavings are little more than dust. Of course, you could use a scraper, but I happen to prefer a plane, because a scraper removes the wood in the form of tendrils, whereas a properly set plane will do the job better and faster most of the time. But a lot depends on the nature and the condition of the wood.

If you are a beginner it is unlikely that you will buy more than one or two general utility bench planes. A good one should last a lifetime. I have a Stanley Jack plane which has been in constant use for years, and apart from a few minor scratches on the body, it is as good as new. The block plane is good enough for most purposes, and I recommend the 6 in. model. The 10 in. smooth plane is always useful for finishing rough surfaces. Beyond these are the speciality planes, such as the scrub plane, for heavy work and the rapid removal of large quantities of wood; the rabbet, which cuts steps in edges for jobs that require tongueing and grooving; the circular plane and spokeshave, which is useful for working on coffee tables, stools and anything with a round or oval shape; the moulding plane with different kinds of interchangeable cutters; and, lastly, the plough, which is used for cutting grooves.

A word of caution . . . many years ago a young lad who was fresh to the world of wood and tools was sent with a blank cheque to buy a plane, and he was instructed to get 'a good one'. Believing 'good' to be synonymous with 'big', he inspected the stock and finally pointed to the biggest one he could see, a 23 in. bull-nosed monster, which nobody wanted. Staggering back with it, he displayed his find and was dryly invited to try pushing it along the edge of a plank. Of course, he couldn't do it, and so he was booted back to the tool factor to find something more manageable. I was the lad and I will not labour the moral of the story.

Many home craftsmen hesitate to buy a combination plane because they look so awkward and difficult to operate, but they are much easier to use than an ordinary block plane. The outlay—the Stanley combination plane costs nearly £6 for the plane itself and the 17 cutters—is small when you reflect that this tool will give you all the uses of the regular plough, plough and dado, adjustable tongueing and regular beading. It is quite possible to panel a room, using only a bandsaw and a combination plane and, perhaps, the Stanley hand router, which cannot be beaten for grooving. I prefer the electric hand router for such jobs, and I shall be discussing this tool later on.

Apart from using all kinds of wood, from fine silky oak to pine, for constructional and decorative use in palaces and pubs for many years, I have from time to time experimented with it for other purposes, including sculpture, using pieces from only three or four inches high to six to ten feet, taking anything from half an hour to more than a year. Contrary to what many people seem to think, wood is far from being a rigid and intractable material. It can be shaped any way you want to shape it so long as you use the right tools. Curves and angles can be cut in such a way as to exploit the grain, and one wood can be laminated to another for the sake of contrast. You can dowel different kinds of wood together so snugly that they look like one piece from a distance of only a few inches. You can take a very cheap wood and stain and finish it so that it looks like expensive maple or the exotic Californian redwood. You can sandblast pine to a finish which leaves the figuring upstanding and removes the softer material. The people who think that making shelves and then screwing them to the wall is the be-all and end-all of working in wood are certainly missing a great deal of pleasure.

My eyes were first opened to the possibilities of

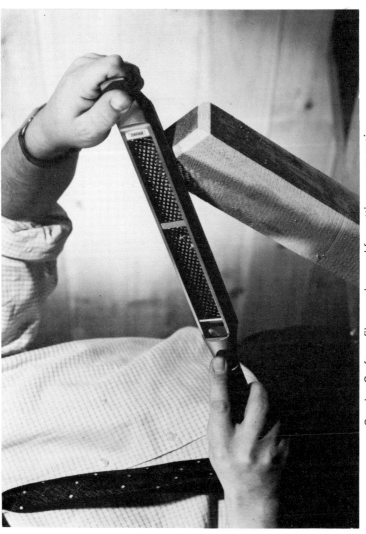

Stanley Surform files can be used for cutting across grain

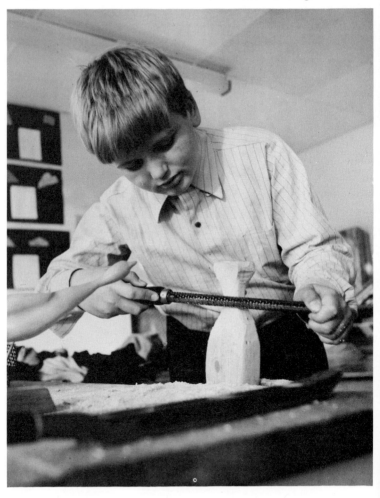

Surform round files are useful for wood sculpture

wood in West Africa before the Second World War, when I was at a place with the improbable name of Cocoa Beach, a steamy river port beyond which we went to Sapeli to load the gargantuan mahogany logs as deck cargo. I was looking for some cold beer in the tin shacks of Cocoa Beach when I noticed an African carving a double-headed dance mask and ornamenting it with animal skins of different colours and textures. It was a life-sized job, full of intricacy and meticulous in all its detail. Seeing me watching him, he stopped work and we talked. His only tool was a much prized double-sided broken file, bastard cut on one side and double-cut on the other, probably picked up at a nearby sawmill many years before. He had ground one end down to a point, and it had no handle. He was a professional carver of great standing in the community and it was his job to carve all the ceremonial masks for his tribe, using just this one tool but achieving amazing versatility.

Wood files and files of other kinds are versatile enough to warrant serious consideration. John Skelton, the nephew of Eric Gill, uses the Surform for some of his wood sculpture, creating the great curved forms which typify his work. Another example can be seen in the work of Michael Smith, a professional carpenter, who also uses the Surform. He has started quite a national movement in our schools and amongst amateurs, who create sculpture of many different kinds. He has also worked with Surform files in other materials, such as Thermalite. A purist would probably say that the Surform is not, in fact, a file at all in the strict sense of the word, but I prefer to classify it on the basis of the *Concise Oxford Dictionary* description of the file as being 'an instrument usually in steel with roughened surface for reducing or smoothing objects'. The Surform is made from rolls of flat steel strip, which is formed to create a series of cutting teeth. These are then ground precisely to the correct angle and height and the blade is corrugated so that the preformed teeth are set at the required angle to avoid a cut which would be much too vicious. The 10 in. blade has more than 400 precision cutting teeth. I have always had a lot of satisfying fun out of my own Surform tools, especially when forming the wings of birds less than half an inch thick at their thinnest point, some shaped in such a way that if a light is put behind them, the figuring of the wood can be seen. The Surform is also a first class tool for working on convex or concave surfaces, because it is quite flexible.

In recent years there have been some interesting mutations of tools for abrading wood. CeKa Tools of North Wales have introduced a kind of twin-edged tool which is formed in a diagonal pattern. It is not unlike six hacksaw blades, rivetted together to make a rigid tool with a handle. It is a new idea and a very good one, because it does not clog, even when you are working on soft wood jobs. CeKa also market a combined gimlet and auger which is useful for working on inside surfaces.

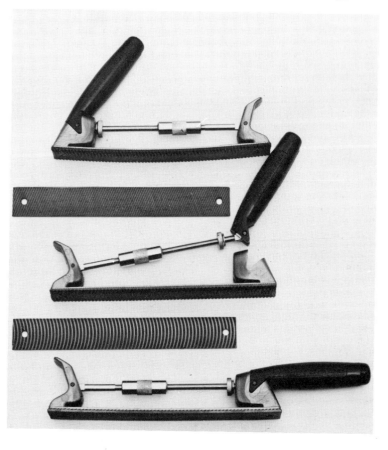

The patent Aven file with a 10 in. blade which can be
used as a plane or file, cutting concave or convex by
tightening the adjustment beam

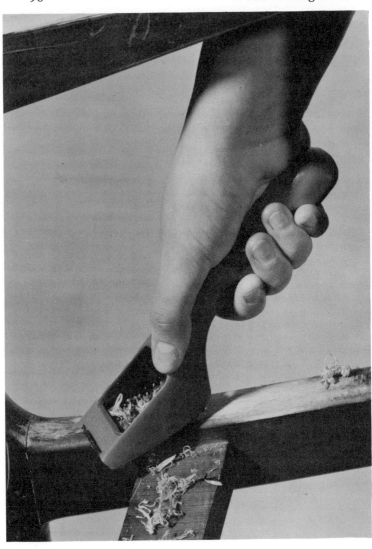

A recently introduced tool—the shaver for smoothing frames and furniture carcases

In the conventional wood file category Aven tools have revived the conventional file with various cuts on either side, and they have also modified the same style for use with a kind of plane tool, incorporating an adjustment so that it can be used in convex or concave positions.

So there is certainly more to the wood file than meets the eye. True, some craftsmen frown on these new ideas, but it should be pointed out that in this department, at least, the end justifies the means. Traditionalists think that it is cheating to use a file to form a rounded corner or smooth off joints. I don't see it that way at all. After all, if you use a chisel to form a rounded corner, there is always the chance of misjudging it and cutting off slightly more than was intended. But if you use a file and shape it very gradually, it will probably be right. I am not, of course, advocating the indiscriminate use of the file or wood rasp. They are tools to be used with the greatest care.

One of my saws is called Septimus. I have a chisel known as Charlie. Tools do have individual personalities, and this certainly applies to files. A new one can be a mule until the teeth have become worn down, and it then changes its attitude and becomes your mate for life. When I acquire a new file, I generally cut down the teeth, using another file, until it runs smoothly. A new one will only chew into the wood and wound it with ridges and furrows which may be difficult to remove. It is an odd thing that two

files made by the same firm from the same batch of
steel with the teeth formed by the same machine can be
quite different in their performance. Of course, a lot
depends on how you use it. Many beginners hold it
only by the handle, whereas the professional way to
hold it is by both ends and have the workpiece at the
right level, which is the height of the elbow. The other
thing to watch is your own position in relation to the
work. Stand away from it so that the forward stroke
will carry enough weight to cut it properly. It takes a
lot of practice to apply weight on the forward cutting .
stroke only and then release it as you withdraw. If the
file is dragged back carelessly, it will only scar and
furrow the wood, but it depends on the type of file you
are using. By varying the angle, you can get different
effects, because files also cut sideways, and the oblique
action can give you a near-smooth surface.

Before looking at the different types of files, I would
just like to mention the rifflers. In silversmithing and
die-making rifflers are used extensively, but they are
not quite as well known in woodworking circles. Apart
from being used on wood, they can also be utilised for
slate and stone sculpture. Their main attraction is that
they are double-ended and with a wide variety of
shapes and various kinds of cut. The longest is 12 in.,
the smallest is 6 in. They are made mainly in Italy and
they are quite expensive, but they are invaluable for
delicate work of many different kinds. One source of
supply in Britain is Alec Tiranti Limited, 72 Charlotte
Street, London, W. 1.

Most of the good tool shops should be able to show you row after row of files, all shapes and sizes and types; round, flat, square, rat-tailed and blunt-ended, from the great 18 in.×2½ in. monster down to the rightly-named mousetail, which is little thicker than wire. At one time you could buy the mousetail file by the yard, but you now get them prepacked and mounted in plastic handles. At one time I used to put a handle on either end to use it like a grocer's cheesecutter, working across the workpiece.

But even if you are stunned by the number of shapes and sizes, the variety of files is covered by some straightforward facts. There are only six different cuts in file making, and they are used to create variations of the main one, which is called the single cut. This consists of a series of teeth, or ridges, cut at an angle. The second type is the double cut, which is the single cut made at two angles in such a way as to create a crisscross pattern. The rasp cut is the third, and it is composed of separate teeth, being used for rough work and the rapid removal of large quantities of wood. Finally, there is the curved cut with spaced teeth.

The second fact to keep in mind is that each of these six cuts is made in seven degrees of coarseness—coarse, bastard, second cut and smooth cut, signified in the trade as Nos. 00, 0, 1, 2, 3, 4, (there is no No. 5) and 6. The actual size of the file does not influence the type of coarseness or smoothness, because these are merely comparative terms. All that happens is an enlargement. Thus, a smooth file of 6 in.

long is the same, in essence, as a file of 12 in., although the teeth will naturally be wider in the large one than in the small one.

Once you understand the grades and the sizes, it is a fairly simple matter to select files for different jobs. What the beginner needs is a selection of cuts in various lengths, including perhaps a half-round rasp, a flat file, a half round one, three or four taper files and a selection of Surforms. Together, they should cover most of your needs. Pillar files can be utilised to smooth down the walls of slots or keyways. Cabinet rasps, as the name implies, are used in furniture making. Round files are best for smoothing rounded surfaces and tapering edges.

A good set of files is a tool set in itself, because if the individual ones are used with thought and care, practically any shaping job can be done. For instance, if I have to make a contoured coffee-table in elm or some other wood, I cut out the shape with the bandsaw, allowing a tolerance of about half an inch all round. The wood is then clamped in a vice, edge uppermost, and tapered all round with a bastard file or a rasp, followed by the finer files, finishing with a Surform or a sander. It is a good idea to use an electric sander to get rid of any sharp edges. Likewise, the bevel of frames can be done with files if no other means exists, although I prefer to cut the bevel on a bandsaw with an adjustable table.

As I mentioned earlier, some very pleasing wood sculpture can be done in all kinds of wood, including the burls or knots which are discarded by sawyers, using only three or four files and Surform.

Dados can be shaped very quickly to resemble antique carving, especially if the dado is shaped with files and then aged by rubbing with sandpaper. If it is open-grained, sieved whiting can be scoured into the grain and the surplus dusted away before varnishing or finishing with button polish to give an unusual and pleasing appearance.

A word here about recent developments. Manufacturers have been trying to develop circular or round files for use with power drills, but apart from the drum-type Surform, they have not been tremendously satisfactory. Having tried out quite a few of these for myself, I have come to the conclusion that it is due to the speed with which they are used. I am referring here not to the mounted steel grinding points but to a straightforward adaptation of the conventional flat file. Where the hand tool is concerned, one can judge the effect to a fraction, but a file which is powered by a powerful electric motor will bite into the wood with such rapidity that it is generally very difficult indeed to keep one eye on the workpiece and the other on the file itself. I suppose you could say that the Abrafile is the best hand-held compromise. It is made to the thickness of substantial steel wire, and is used by clamping it in an ordinary hacksaw frame in conjunction with spring link or plain adaptors. Abrafiles can be obtained in lengths of 6 in., 8 in., and 11 in. in coarse, medium and fine grades. The obvious advantage of this type of file is that you can thread it through an inside surface, just the same as a mousetail, and then use it as one uses a fretsaw, the teeth being non-clogging. I must admit that when I first started using the Abrafile, I was impatient with what seemed to be very slow progress until it finally dawned on me that the frame tension was too slack. If Abrafiles are properly used, however, rapid progress can be made. On one occasion I went clean through the end of my fingernail while steadily filing and turning to say thank-you to my wife for a mug of tea.

7   Boring tools

Boring through wood can be done in many different ways, the most basic method being to bash a six inch nail straight through the timber, withdraw it and then thread a fretsaw and cut the hole to the required dimensions. It is, of course, grossly inelegant to do things like this. Equally, an iron can be heated and the hole burned out, the charring being removed with a tapered file. This, too, is inelegant and it also stinks. A few years ago in North Wales I saw a young craftsman working with a piece of sharpened slate, using it to bore holes with great speed and accuracy. He had only recently started as a self-employed craftsman because his quarry had closed down. As he walked out on his last day, he happened to pick up a length of slate which he made into a hole maker.

Boring tools were evolved in ancient Egypt, probably as a natural improvement on the earlier methods of tying or lashing pieces of wood together. Many early ocean-going craft were literally tied together like this and Thor Heyerdahl's recent experiments with his papyrus boat, Ra, have shown that the method has much to commend it. It is likely that the hole-making tool first took the form of an awl, but man's constant search for improvement and innovation led to the evolution of the bow drill. During the two thousand years of ancient Egyptian civilisation, craftsmen started making dowels for the construction of buildings, especially for the inner partitions, the main fabric being of stone. Dowels were also used for the making of sarcophagi. It is simple enough to date the bow drill, because the sarcophagi can be seen in museums throughout the world. An approximate date for the introduction of the bow drill would be about 2540 BC, and it continued in an unbroken line through to the Middle Ages, giving it one of the longest lineages of the non-specialist tools. It is an odd thing that some tools will enjoy thousands of years of popularity and then abruptly drop from view for no apparent reason. This happened to the bow drill, but it did come back, and the Romans used it for many years. In the end it was supplanted by the breast auger and the brace, both faster and more powerful. Yet it seems that the bow drill cannot be kept down. It did return and it is still with us.

The main line of development begins with the auger, probably long before the dynasties of ancient Egypt. It always consisted of a pointed metal shank and some kind of handle. The auger which can be bought from any tool shop in our own time is not very different from the auger of *c.* 1329 which can be seen in the Antikritersakademien at Stockholm. In ancient times the tool was in common use, and it appears frequently in such documents as have come down to us. Spoon-ended augers were used to make holes for cathedral furnishings, when large reredos had to be assembled after the carver had finished his work. Reredos—ornamental screens behind altars—were made up to twenty feet or more in height, and so it was not practical to put them together flat on the floor of the nave and then manhandle them into position. Thus, when the first was upright, the craftsman climbed up the light scaffolding with the auger and the dowels while his assistants used ropes to haul the neighbouring section into position under the direction of the carver, and by the time it reached the assembler, the auger had been used to make the holes, and the dowels could then be rammed home. The new section was halted within reach of the assembler, who then used an auger to make the mating holes. From what we know of these medieval reredos, it was not unusual to apply hundreds of dowels to hold the tall screen upright. On completion, it was braced as a rule with side irons and floor brackets which were then cemented over and concealed from view.

Ancient augers have a pointed end, but others have a spoon bit, which provided a reaming action. They were used widely not only in the construction of ecclesiastical and secular furniture but also in such trades as shipbuilding and wagon making. The limitations of the hand auger are obvious, because it is governed entirely by the hand and the arm, and it takes skill to cut, say, a $\frac{1}{4}$ in. to $\frac{1}{2}$ in. hole and remove the plug of wood cleanly without breaking it. The ancient craftsman probably felt the same way about it, and he went on his way, grumbling down the centuries about the inadequacy of the tool. More power was needed, because it would give greater accuracy. Even in those days they had their productivity problems. While the basic principle of the auger was right, the search was on for more power, and so the innovators of those days eventually produced the breast drill, which is still in use in various parts of Europe, particularly Sweden. It consists of the auger bit which is fitted into a long handle and is, itself, equipped with handles. The butt of the handle is held against the chest while the point rests on the workpiece, and the handles are then turned while leaning against the butt. In this way it became possible to regulate the pressure. The modern wood drill is, of course, a natural development of this principle with its shoulder brace and the cranking action. The brace was in common use as early as the fifteenth century.

The modern brace was introduced about 1864 with the adjustable jaws and a shell-type chuck. Apart from a few refinements in the various aspects of design, there have been very few revolutionary changes. To-day's version is very easy to use and, apart from its main use as a hole maker, it will, with the aid of special bits, also act as a screwdriver, a countersinker, and it will cut dowel housings and do many other jobs. At between £2 and £4 it is a useful investment.

When you buy a brace, keep the size in mind. They are sized in 'sweeps'. A sweep is the diameter of the revolution of the brace, the commonest being 8 in., 10

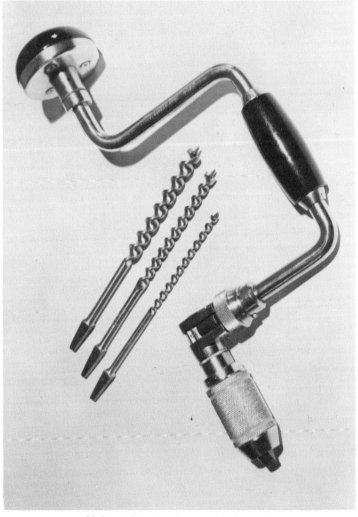

Universal ratchet brace with three bits

in., and 14 in., costing from £2·95 up to £4·10. A set of bits, thirteen in all, from $\frac{1}{4}$ in. up to 1 in. in sixteenths of an inch will cost about £13, but this is a once and for all investment. You can also buy adjustable bits with separate cutters, but they tend to be expensive and they are not always satisfactory when working to fine limits.

I was brought up on a combination of what you might call 'Get that ruddy floor swept' and brace and bit practice. The last decade or two have seen some changes, dictated mainly by sheer economics, because when you have to cut holes in oak or teak or other hardwoods and the job is being priced on time rather than results, it is more profitable to plug in a power tool and let the electric motor do the donkey work for you. I admit that a hole is still a hole whichever way you look at it, but there is still more satisfaction to be gained from doing it by hand.

Apart from the brace and bit there are other ways of making clean holes in wood. For instance, there is the hand drill, which can be obtained in two-speed models. Some very well designed models are available to take $\frac{1}{4}$ in. drills, costing as little as £2, and practically all of them are fitted with the three-jaw chuck. It is not unusual for the beginner to buy one only to find at his first attempt that the point of the drill slips and jerks about. One chap I know tried to drive the drill into the wood with a hammer. While he was very roughly on the right lines, he should have used an awl to make a small hole to provide purchase for the drill. Once this

Hand drill suitable for all kinds of boring operations. It uses $\frac{1}{4}$ in. drills and a standard chuck

has been obtained and an even speed is maintained, the drill should pierce quite evenly. Dependent on the thickness of the material being drilled, it is a good idea to withdraw the drill from the hole now and then to clear the debris, otherwise the going can get harder and harder. The secret of successful drilling is not to go at it in fits and starts or tackle it in a do-or-die attempt but to maintain a firm pressure.

The pressure should always be directly downwards, because if there is even the slightest deviation, the drill will begin to move on the skew, and the angle will increase. In some cases, when drilling hardwood, this may even snap the drill. Some interesting research has been done on drills under tension, and it appears that breakage is caused by a combination of generated frictional heat and the gradual 'bowing' of the drill when it is operated out of true. I have seen tensile steel drills bow like violin strings when the pressure is too great. If this happens to a power drill, there is, of course, a considerable danger of the pieces of metal flying up in the face, but no such hazard exists with the hand-operated version.

With constant wear even the best drill becomes blunt. It might seem impossible to sharpen the corkscrew shape, but it is, in fact, no harder than it is to sharpen an ordinary straight chisel. Drills are prone to chipping, and so they should be stored in a roll of oiled flannel when not in use. As far as sharpening is concerned, you can buy a small jig in which the drill is mounted in successive stages and sharpened. There is also available an angle measurer to check that a constant angle has been maintained. The measurer is called a twist drill point gauge.

The other ancillary aid is a depth gauge to enable you to drill holes to an equal depth. There is a favourite trick played on the naïve apprentice, who is told to drill twenty holes of equal depth but different diameters in a piece of wood. I once watched two likely lads tackling this exercise, and their antics went on all morning to the delight of the fiendish master carpenter who was pulling their legs. The first lad foolishly measured off the depth of the hole on the shank of the drill, using an engineer's file to notch it and, of course, imperceptibly weakening the steel. Granted, he did make a fair job of his holes and they were all more or less uniform in depth, although the method by which he achieved this result would not have earned him a City and Guilds pass. The second lad was ingeniously obvious in his method. He drilled a bit at a time and then poked a piece of wire down the hole and measured the length. Seventeen of his holes were too deep. Both lads were irritated and puzzled to know how it was possible to drill holes to a predetermined depth until their mentor fixed a little rubber ring at a certain point on the drill shank. It was a piece cut from an ordinary valve rubber for pushbike tyres.

8 Saws

Perhaps the most bizarre incident involving saws which ever happened to me occurred when I was working not in wood but in the field of medical specimen preparation for a hospital laboratory and medical museum. My boss, now deceased, was an excitable Viennese surgeon, and anything new in the way of tools or techniques never failed to fascinate him, although he was not a practical man.

One of my main tasks was to prepare dozens of specimens of human bone. This necessitated sawing the long bones of the legs and arms and creating discs so that my bench looked like a croupier's table. To do this properly I used a surgical version of the tenon saw. It did not suit my boss, who complained that production was slow, and the discs were either too thick or too thin for exhibition and demonstration purposes. Despite my opposition, he badgered the hospital into buying an ordinary power drill and an equally ordinary circular saw, which arrived totally naked and without a guard of any kind. He slammed these prizes down on my bench. We argued for a week about it. I refused point blank to even try it until he was goaded into doing it himself. He savagely jammed the plug in the socket and switched on, then attacked the bone with the saw. Within a few seconds he had a face full of bone splinters. The berserk drill skuttered towards me until I clobbered it with a towel. Then I went back to my hand saw.

That reminds me of a comical incident in which a friend of mine in the building trade was working on a high roof, using a power saw of ancient years which had a habit of switching itself on without human intervention. He had just finished cutting a plank of wood and laid the tool down when it started up and began to run about in all directions. He was seriously thinking of jumping for it when it slashed through its own power cable and expired in a shower of sparks and a short circuit.

But in the general run of things, saws are pretty harmless tools. The first saw was probably a long narrow piece of flint or some other natural material with rough serrations chipped into it. Flint knappers of our own time, who make reproduction arrowheads, hammerheads and other examples of Stone Age tools, tell me that it is quite easy to fashion a flint saw capable of cutting through a three inch thickness of softwood, and while the results may not approach modern standards for cleanness of cut, the fact remains that it can be done. When the world did not have any metal, what more natural than for primitive man to create flint saws and then lash them to wooden handles? The saw probably came later than hunting implements, enabling primitive man to cut tree branches to the right size and build wooden racks on

which the meat could be stored. And so the first
kitchen units were created! Examples of the flint saw
dating back to Neolithic times have survived, being
found in Europe, Egypt and what is now known as
Israel. Archaeological opinion about their precise use
varies, because some authorities call them long
knives. I think this is yet another example of under-
estimating the mind of Neolithic man, because
he was quite capable of working out the idea of the
saw for himself. Other archaeological opinion has it
that these are knives with serrated edges, which were
used for cutting up meat or for cutting round animal
bone before giving it a clout with a stone hammer to
make a clean break and taking the weekend joint home.

Metal saws materialised in the Early Bronze Age,
and some remarkably 'modern' looking examples
dating back to about 1490 BC can be seen in the
British Museum. One of them is twenty inches long
with a pointed tang for the fitting of a handle. This and
others were found in Egypt and the metal is said to be
copper. The ancient frieze is of help here, for it shows
that saws were known to the Egyptians for at least two
thousand years. Saw making was a regular industry in
ancient Egypt. We know this from the remarkable
uniformity of the specimens which have been found.
However, the tool maker of those days forged and cut
hooked teeth, the hooks running back towards the
handle to give a tearing or ripping action. When a
tomb was being opened in the Valley of the Kings an
archaeologist came on a small piece of wood in a

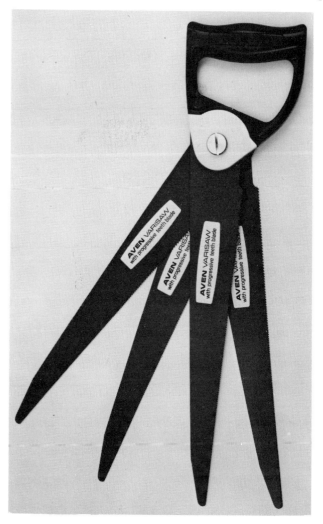

Many saws are now sold with 'nests' of blades for a variety of uses

corner which had apparently been used on several sides to test a saw, because the marks were as fresh as the day they were made. The archaeologist-critics have said that the saws of this period must have been inefficient. Be that as it may you need only examine the tomb furniture in all its elegance at the Cairo Museum of Antiquities to see how wrong they are.

The development of the saw was fairly constant. Some interesting comparisons can be made. For instance, a saw discovered at Krasnoyar in Siberia is unusual in that it has two serrated edges, while a specimen found at Llynfawr, Glamorgan, is practically the same. Exactly how the exchange of technical information was made across thousands of miles we do not know.

The Romans introduced the saw frame, influenced quite possibly by the Greek design, some specimens of which can be seen in Moscow Museum. They go back to the tenth century. I must admit that I have for many years been mystified by the reason for the design and the introduction of the frame saw, because you would naturally imagine that the most logical development would be a refinement of the all-metal saw with the handgrip, much as we know it. At a moment in history somebody elected to mount a thin strip of toothed metal inside a tensioned frame, perhaps with the notion of it being worked by two sawyers, one at either end to hasten the job. Moreover, rigidity of the saw blade would be achieved, giving greater accuracy when sawing curves. The archaic frame saw is now known as the joiner's bow saw, or turning saw, and in design it differs very little from those in use in Roman times, although the Roman model had the blade mounted in the middle of the frame. It was probably used for rip sawing long lengths, the wood resting on a high frame so that one sawyer could stand underneath and the other on top. The method of tensioning the blade was just the same in Roman times as now, namely by means of a twisted cord and a peg which could be turned and then wedged against the frame. The modern bow saw is a joy to use, because it is both light and balanced, and it will cut to the finest limits with a minimum of effort after a certain amount of practice. It is available in a number of sizes, including 8 in., 10 in., 12 in., 14 in., and 16 in.

Just as civilisations can be measured by the development of their art forms, so entire cultures can be evaluated on the strength of their tools. Many civilisations which are only half known to us had as ready a grasp of toolmaking as we have. In the jungles of South America there are traces of exceptionally well developed civilisations with evidence—primarily in the form of stone cutting—which show that saws were designed, made and powered by hand and they were in advance of some of our modern tools. The great monoliths on Easter Island were first of all sawn out of a quarry or a cliff face before the sculptors used hammer and chisel to hew out those massive and impassive heads which blindly stare out over thousands of miles of lonely ocean.

In the centuries which followed the end of the
Roman Empire a kind of technological Dark Age
persisted. From being comparatively well-developed
and balanced, tools became clumsy and ill-designed.
The hallmark of Anglo-Saxon times was a universal
clumsiness. This applied particularly to saws, which
were thick and with wider teeth than before. But even
this murky epoch managed to yield something,
because the handsaw emerged. Just the other day I
treated myself to an Eclipse saw with a multiple
positioning adjustment device and a blade which can
be used on wood or metal. Although it was promoted
as the 'very latest' in saw design, it is actually less than
five seconds away from medieval saws if we want to
think in terms of tool evolution.

It would probably be possible to write an entire
book about the saw and the way it has played a vital
part in man's development. In the same way, the
woodyards where we buy our materials are the direct
descendants of the sawyers' establishments of medieval times, when the great beams of churches and
cathedrals were roughed out and prefabricated, and
then finished on site. Although the 'modern' system
uses the prefabrication of doors, roof trusses and window frames, the method is essentially the same in that
all the preliminary sawing and shaping is done miles
away from the place where the results will be
incorporated in the building.

A good saw should last for more than fifty years
and so it should be selected with the greatest care. The

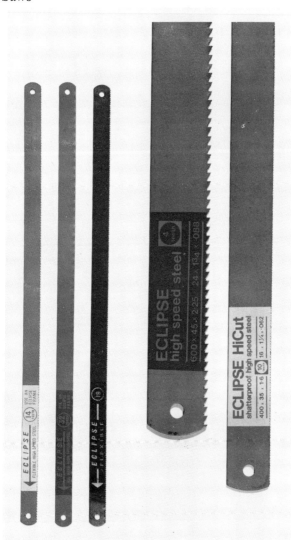

A selection of hacksaw blades

cheaper saws—generally imported from Hong Kong—are treated with contempt by wholesalers and retailers alike, and they are thrown on shelves or tossed into racks. In the course of this rough treatment the teeth may become buckled or bent. Good saws, on the other hand, are always packed in stout individual boxes or fitted with strong teeth guards, and they are handled with care. When you buy your first saw, it should be a utility crosscut of a size which you can handle without fatigue. It is pointless buying the biggest you can find because, if you happen to be a short person with short arms, you will soon wear yourself out if you have to use it for any length of time. Another point to watch out for is the handle. In the Plastic Age, even saw handles are made of this material, which is indestructible. I still prefer the wooden handle because it absorbs sweat, whereas a plastic one soon becomes slippery and has to be wiped every few minutes.

The crosscut saw is easily tested by standing it with the teeth uppermost and a thin sewing needle resting between the teeth, the point towards the end, or toe, of the saw. If the saw is slightly tilted, the needle should slide smoothly all the way down. If just one tooth is out of alignment the needle will stop, and that is the saw to be put back on its hook. A good general utility crosscut will have between eight and ten teeth to the inch.

You will probably discover a need for several different kinds of saw. After the crosscut, a good

Hand and back saws, plain steel and Teflon coated

choice is a tenon saw for cutting joints, and it will have between fourteen and eighteen teeth to the inch in the 12 in. to 16 in. size. Yet another one is the compass saw, long and tapered, and with blades for cutting on the curve. The coping saw is also used for cutting curves, but on a much smaller scale. I have discovered a coping saw to be useful for all kinds of work, especially plywood. The steel-framed hacksaw also has many uses, and it does not cost much.

Saws need sharpening. This happens to be one of those little services which has practically disappeared, so it has to be a do-it-yourself operation. The first thing to decide is the point where the saw becomes blunt, and this is shown by a kind of smoothness in the cutting when the teeth seem to be losing their bite. This is the point at which the saw needs sharpening. There is a standard way of doing this, based on the number of points to the inch. The following table shows which files should be used:

$4\frac{1}{2}$, $5\frac{1}{2}$, 6	use 7 in. slim taper file
7, 8	use 6 in. slim taper file
11, 12, 13, 14, 15	use $4\frac{1}{2}$ in. slim taper file
16 or more	use 5 in. superfine metal saw file, cut no. 2

The first part of the sharpening operation involves inspecting the teeth. If they are all of equal height, this stage can be by-passed, although it is likely that some teeth will be higher than others. It is very important

Multiple purpose saw with short handle for sawing, slitting, slotting, scribing

that all the teeth are of the same height, and so they must be filed down in order to level them out. This is done by sandwiching the blade between two pieces of wood with the teeth just showing. If a lot of the teeth have become irregular, you should file from the top, flattening out all the points and levelling them. Before doing this it is advisable to examine the teeth which are close to the handle to find out the way the pitch runs.

Using the correct file, as above, and working at the right angle in relation to the saw, lightly file each tooth. At this stage it is unnecessary to worry about the bevel, because this is done later. The important thing is to put a new cutting edge on the tooth itself. If the correct file is being used, it is much easier than it seems in print. The beginner is advised to take it easy, not putting on too much pressure unless he wants the tooth to disappear completely. The work should be examined through a magnifying glass at frequent intervals to ensure that a good even edge is being achieved. The best angle at which to work is 45 degrees, although this varies from saw to saw.

When all the teeth have been filed, the saw should be placed in its wooden sandwich in the vice with the handle on the righthand side. The first tooth which is pointing towards you should be filed, and, thereafter, each alternate one. When all the alternate teeth have been filed, the saw should be reversed. This means that the handle will now be on the lefthand side. The entire process is then repeated. And that is all there is to it. It takes time, but it rejuvenates the saw.

An all-purpose saw with a seven-position blade

Steel-framed hacksaw

The short answer is that power tools can do almost anything. Every year the designers can be counted on to produce new attachments, although the basic principle of the power unit does not alter. In effect, power tools are just ordinary hand tools modified, mechanised and powered to make them suitable for all kinds of work. The only difference is in technique, because power tool working is something which must be learned, and in the learning a great deal of quite expensive wood can be reduced to chips. A good analogy is the manual typewriter and its electrical counterpart, which is said to remove about one-third of the muscular effort needed to put the words on the paper on the manual machine. Of course, some people just cannot get on with power tools any more than some typists can get on with electric machines. Like my friend Simpson, who realised the ambition of a lifetime and bought himself a beautiful wood turning lathe. Simpson was blatantly middle-class and he worked in the City, and so he naturally wore a tie at all times. The day his lathe arrived, he delightedly put on what he called his 'working togs', including dungarees and a sporty-looking shirt with a knitted tie. He had no trouble at all in setting up the lathe and all its gadgets, and he then started roughing out a bowl. Within a few moments his tie was caught up and his face thrust dangerously close to the spinning workpiece. He just about managed to reach the switch in time. So Simpson learned the first and most basic answer to what power tools can do. They can decapitate you if you give them half a chance. The other things they can do is bore a hole through your finger in a few seconds. They can also electrocute you.

Nearly all power tools have multiple applications. However, beware of the machine which the cheaper manufacturers claim will 'do anything and everything', because it is often flimsy and it takes far too long to set up, so in the end it defeats its own ingenuity. But this does not by any means apply to all multiple-use machines. For instance, the De Walt Power Shop, sold in Britain by Black and Decker but made in America, has 15 different applications, including a radial power saw, dado tool, tilt arbor shaper, horizontal drill router, surfacer, grinder, jointer, drum sander, disc sander, sabre saw, buffer polisher and metal cutting rebater. Similarly, the Myford ML8 has facilities for power sawing, planing, bandsawing, mortising, routing, grooving, polishing, grinding, long boring, metal turning and metal spinning.

The economics of multiple tools like these are at first sight pretty daunting to the man of limited means, an average price range being between £150 and £300 with some extras, which can cost £50 or more if you want to go the whole hog. It represents a considerable outlay, even when paid in instalments, so if you are sensible you should first of all weigh up exactly how much use the machine will have. It is quite remarkable how much impulse buying there is in this bracket. Some people buy them like women buy knitting machines and then, after making a few garments, put them away under the bed to gather dust. One fellow paid nearly £200 for a multi-purpose set-up, and all he made was six oak bowls, two doors, a dog kennel and some elaborate shelves. The machine was then covered up and left to rot simply because the owner could not think what next to make with it.

If you buy one of these machines, it is essential to use it for one basic purpose. For instance, if you are self-employed, you might produce table lamps and other merchandise for gift shops or a wholesaler. Similarly, some long-run repetition jobs can be done for different industries in certain areas of the country. There used to be a profitable business in producing wooden discs or blocks for electrical switch manufacturers, but this vanished with the introduction of moulded plastic housings. A relative of mine bought one of these machines and landed a profitable contract to make tapered wooden stoppers for ornamental rum bottles. In another direction he produced picture frames for private customers and soon had more orders than he could manage. In such a case the machine obviously pays for itself in less than a couple of years. But the idea of getting such a machine for the occasional domestic job is absolutely ludicrous and a sheer waste of time and money. But for the compulsive woodworker who regularly makes furniture, decides to build an annexe to the house, a patio or some other major items, then one of these units can be invaluable. I know of one instance of six unemployed miners deciding to build a palatial bungalow to their own design, and they somehow managed to rake up enough cash to pay for a secondhand machine. With it they made all the constructional woodwork plus the fitted furniture and, later, a lot more furniture for the place. It took three years to build and they eventually sold it for £12,000.

So what are the drawbacks to a multiple purpose unit? None at all, providing you can find enough work for it to do. Perhaps the only drawback is an aesthetic one, concerning the noise. With such a hefty chunk of machinery you can hardly expect a low hum. The neighbours will complain about the vibration, which might be transmitted through the floorboards, joists and plumbing. This is not necessarily noisy, but it can be irritating, especially in flats and semi-detached houses. While most of the multiple purpose units are not half as bad as smaller tools, like power drills and routers, they still create a persistent and penetrating noise, apart from which the noise of whatever operation is being carried out can make a whining, grinding or plain noisy row. It just cannot be avoided, although some precautions for minimising it can be observed, especially when the work area is used regularly as a workshop. The best way of doing this is by using rolls of fibreglass wool insulating material and laying it against the walls, then covering it with chipboard, pegboard or blockboard. Solid chipboard is best. Bearing in mind that sound and vibration are transmitted through permanent fittings, it is a good idea to use rubber grommets where the battens are screwed into position. As far as an alternative to wall facing is concerned, I can recommend cork sheets, although they are often expensive. There are various fibreboard and plasterboard products, which are just as good and much cheaper.

The principle of noise generation is easy to understand. When you attach a noise maker, such as a power drill or a router, to a flat surface, the noise will travel in a series of waves into and through the material. If nothing can be attached to the walls to make an inner skin, then some heavy drapes will help to deaden it. Another material is plywood, but it is expensive. I have also seen egg-box separators used, although they act as a dust trap. Ideally, when you insulate a room, you should try and create a room within a room, but if this is out of the question, then it should be possible to use portable screening, which can be placed round the working area.

Once the room or working area has been treated, there remains the question of fixed tools, such as grinders, lathes, table saws and drill presses, which are screwed permanently to benches. The amount of vibration which is generated can be tremendous in comparison to the size of the tool itself, but it can be drastically reduced by setting the tool down on a bed of rubber or neoprene about $\frac{1}{2}$ to $\frac{3}{4}$ of an inch thick. It can be made doubly effective if the rubber is sandwiched between thin metal plates, but this is not strictly necessary, although it helps the stability. It is essential that the tool is screwed down very tightly, compressing the rubber to its maximum extent. Some people insulate only the feet of the tool, but this is insufficient, because the vibrations pass through the entire area of the bed. The other sound reducer is located in the feet of the bench itself or whatever the bench rests on. Here again, rubber or neoprene is used, this time in the form of blocks and angle irons, which are used to hold the structure to the floor.

Although I have been suggesting that noise reduction is in the interests of others, it is also beneficial to you, because the effects of noise can be considerable. Just try working in the middle of a sustained whine for hour after hour, and you will soon see how it frays the nerves.

There is no more portable and versatile power tool than the drill. It can be used with various attachments for such jobs as conventional drilling, mortising, sanding, sawing; it can be used for cutting rebates, rapers, mouldings; and it can also be used as an orbital sander, and for all kinds of grinding and for polishing wood and metal. When attached to a lathe bed, it is useful for turning small wooden articles, such as table and chair legs, and bowls. Used with a flexible drive, it can be used for work which is difficult to reach.

In the bad old days a lot of people were electrocuted when they used cheap and shoddy power drills. They were full of wiring defects. They wore out quickly. It took government intervention to halt the sale of these death traps. Nowadays the quality of manufacture must conform to the strictest standards. But, at the same time, you have to remember that when you are holding a power tool in your hand, what you have is a piece of machinery through which electricity is flowing, and so all the usual precautions must be observed which apply to any piece of electrically powered machinery. There should be no dampness in the vicinity—and that is rule one. Taking into account that the drill is generally moved about, there is a lot of play at two points, namely where the lead enters the drill housing and at the plug end. It is a good idea to have plenty of lead available to allow for this play, and the two danger areas should be inspected every time the tool is used. Once deterioration does start, it can be rapid. Of course, you should have the drill serviced regularly by the manufacturers or an agent.

There is a system of classifying electric drills, and it is by the size of the chuck. The usual sizes are $\frac{1}{4}$ in. and $\frac{5}{16}$ in., and these relate to the smaller models for domestic and home workshop use. But to my mind

Power drills fitted with a grinding wheel for tool sharpening can be fitted to the bench with a metal clamp-holder

there is a lot to be said for investing in one of the much larger and more powerful industrial models, which are built to withstand a lot of rough handling.

Although Wolf Electrical Tools Ltd (Pioneer Works, Hanger Lane, London, W 5) produce light electric drills, I have been very impressed by their industrial models and in particular by the special attention which the firm has paid to the safety factor. A considerable number of fatal accidents are still connected with the earthing systems of drills. There have been many instances where a complete lack of earthing has caused the accident, when a fault has developed in the appliance and the current has returned to earth via the operator. There are the cases where the three-core cable has been connected up with the earth wire to one of the power terminals and has made the whole body of the machine live. It will be appreciated that without a check on the earthing system every time an appliance is used, it is not possible to know whether there is earthing continuity. The problem of earthing has now led to the development of, firstly, double insulated tools and, in the case of the Wolf series, all-insulated drills. With only a two-cord cable, it is impossible to wire it up incorrectly. Indeed, if one of the wires did happen to be connected to the earth terminal on the plug, the machine just would not function and there would be no danger to the operator. In October 1968 a Statutory order was issued to the Factory Inspectorate which allowed the use of non-earthed tools on industrial premises when they carry a recognised certification, such as the BSI Kite Mark. This was the first alteration to the electrical regulations contained in the Factories Act of 1908 and it was long overdue. The additional operator-safety offered by these tools was recognised on the Continent much earlier than it was in Britain. For instance, in Holland it is law that only double-insulated tools and all-insulated tools shall be used on industrial premises, and in many other countries their use is recommended by the authorities.

Over the years great attention has been paid to the development of the two-speed and three-speed electric drill. Nowadays, most of them are two-speed with a speed of about 20,000 rpm on the armature main shaft which is geared down to around 3,000 rpm. In some models the circulation of air is directed through a frontal duct to clear debris while drilling. In the last

couple of years variable speed reducers have come on
the market, and they cost about £5. By using one of
these you can reduce drill speed to almost zero. Slow
speed drilling is particularly useful for working many
materials where it is desirable to avoid a build-up of
frictional heat in the cutting area and in the drilling
head itself. For instance, a $\frac{1}{4}$ in. drill can be used to
bore a hole through mild steel with a speed reduction
ratio of 7 to 1. Some recent power drills incorporate a
speed reducer, but this is not yet common practice,
and those on the market are pretty expensive. One of
the benefits of the reducer is that it has opened up
many new uses for drills. For instance, you can now
work with different materials, including glass, the
technique being to form a clay or Plasticine wall
around the drilling area and fill it with turpentine,
which acts as a lubricant to prevent breakage. The
speed should be dead slow and the drilling pressure
gradual. When drilling glass, it is a good idea to use a
drill press in which pressure is more controlled than in
hand drilling. When you drill any material, it is good
policy to start with low r.p.m., gradually speeding up
as the characteristics of the material are observed. This
avoids overloading the motor. When too much strain
is imposed on it, fatter blue sparks will be seen through
the vents. They originate at the point where the
brushes are in contact with the commutator. It can
also cause overheating. If the drill has been running
for twenty minutes or more, the casing will probably
be hot anyway, and if you are concentrating on the job

in hand, it may go unnoticed. The moral is, don't run
the drill for long periods at full speed. Like a horse, it
needs a rest now and then.

One of the neglected uses for a drill is the shaping
and contouring of wood, using rotary files. Many of
the standard rotary files can be modified by grinding
down, enabling you to work at angles and in corners
which can't be reached with ordinary tools. One point
to remember when doing work of this sort is the
amount of wrist tension and the pressure needed to
hold the tool to the workpiece. If you are working with
the grain, the tool will have a tendency to skitter away,
but if you are working against the grain and cutting
sharply into the wood, the tool will chatter and jump
about. Either way, this can be very dangerous. To
avoid accidents, the work must be firmly clamped and
the tool itself held with both hands.

Practically all electric drills can be clamped into
steel stands which are themselves bolted to the bench.
By this means it is possible to attach circular wire
brushes, grinding wheels and other devices which have
many uses in home workshops.

In another application the drill will form the basis of
a saw table, the table itself being bought separately
with a mitreing attachment, which makes it possible to
do jobs like sawing at precise angles. Most tables are
equipped with a rip fence and extensions can be added
to enlarge their scope.

While scroll work can be carved with the
appropriate tools or even rough sawn by hand and

then finished with files, there is the point that this kind of work can become very tedious. The answer is a jigsaw attachment to the power drill. By this means circular, irregular and straight cuts can be made with the greatest ease. Most jigsaws include a rod guide and a radius rod for circular work.

Sawing plays an important part in any workshop, although many of the do-it-yourself manuals and articles in magazines generally include cutting lists, and so the enthusiast takes these lists to the timber yard and has the pieces supplied practically ready for assembling. Of course, there is nothing against doing this, but it can be expensive, because the timber yards do not do the work for nothing. After all, it takes time to set up a saw, study the list, sort out the wood and so on and so forth. I have known cases of some people taking their cutting lists to the experts while their own expensive saws stood idly at home. Maybe this is a form of self-punishment for all the money they have wasted on tools which they do not understand and cannot handle. After all, it takes about fifty seconds to hand saw a piece of 2×4 timber, given a nice cool day and a steady stroke. On the other hand, if you use an electric saw, you should get through the same piece of wood in about three seconds flat. Now, apply these times to multiple cutting. If you are making uprights for ranch fencing for the garden, it is likely that marking the wood will take longer than the sawing. The same applies to cutting mitres. A mitre can be cut by hand in about one and a half minutes. An electric saw takes less than ten seconds.

The first experiments with a power saw will seem very satisfying, because all the muscular fag is removed. All you have to do is push the revolving saw against the wood if you are using a power drill attachment, or feed the wood into the saw if you are using a radial arm saw or a table saw. When the saw is new, it will slice through the wood at a great rate, giving out an alarming scream. As soon as it is worn in, it will let out a contented zizzing.

Power saws will be dealt with separately. What we are concerned with at the moment are saw attachments to the power drill. Frankly, I do not care for these, because of all operations sawing can be the most dangerous, and I think that the saw should be an entirely separate unit. Obviously, if the jaws of the drill are worn, there is a very real danger of the saw flying off at an angle and catching you a fourpenny one in the face or the hand, even when you are taking precautions. It is incredible that some otherwise quite sane and sensible people will use a naked circular saw without any guard on it, and yet if they saw this being done in a commercial workshop or a factory, they would puff up with indignation. The safety regulations which govern the use of tools in industry should apply in the home, especially when small children are present.

A few years ago the flexidrive was made available for use with power drills and the price came down with a thud. In some cases, so did the quality. This often happens, because there are just as many get-rich-quick boys in tool manufacture as elsewhere. The main faults are bad wiring, casings which crack because they are brittle in the first place, and a lack of motor power. In flexidrives the flaws consist as a rule of jamming when the cable is bent beyond a slight curve, sluggishness during ordinary operating conditions and, lastly, a loss of power. Then there are the chucks, which are made from cast metal or soft metal. They either fall off or else they disintegrate after a few weeks or months. In some shops they will let you test a flexidrive by attaching it to a power drill and then switching on. It should then slowly but surely be bent to find out whether there is any slowing up or loss of power. The new flexidrive will be rather stiff to begin with and due allowance should be made for this. I generally run a small quantity of lubricating oil through the inside of the drive and leave it hanging up overnight to let it seep through.

There are some unusual uses for flexidrives, which come in a variety of different lengths, the commonest being 3 ft 6 in. with a shaft diameter of $\frac{3}{8}$ in. and a drill chuck of $\frac{1}{4}$ in. shank on the driving end. Both ends are fitted with hand grips. One of the greatest facilities offered by the flexidrive is its ability to get into corners, where it would be very difficult to use a power drill. They are also useful for preparing furniture for re-finishing, and wonders can be worked with a fairly soft wire brush or an abrasive disc when it is a matter of getting into nooks and crannies. You can go on working for hours with a flexidrive, whereas if you tried to do it with a power drill in your hand, you would probably flake out after an hour or so. Probably the most versatile artist with a flexidrive and other power drill attachments is Ralph E. Byers, an American, who wrote a book I can recommend, *Wood Carving with Power Tools* (Pitman, 1959).

If you have done much sandpapering by hand, you will be familiar with that sensation of the aching back and arm muscles as you rub away to try and achieve an overall smoothness. If you use a wood or cork block, your fingers soon become cramped. If you do not use a block, you find that your fingers have gone through the stuff and you end up with a fine crop of painful blisters. I do not deny that sandpapering is a fine and manly job for strapping apprentices, but for those who want to avoid martyrdom, the power drill can be a real godsend. It is useful to have a few test runs on some scrap wood before working on anything of value. The reason for this is that you have an abrasive disc revolving at about 2,000 rpm against wood, and it will bite into it so rapidly that in no time some shallow dips and curves will appear. When sanding, the tool must be kept on the move in sweeping or circular movements, otherwise it will cut sharply into places where no sanding is needed. This applies particularly to the rigid discs, but others can be obtained which consist of a flexible rubber disc over which the abrasive pad fits. When this revolves at a high speed, it is possible to achieve a delicacy of touch for smoothing down even the most delicate work. Power sanding of this sort is not, admittedly, very easy, but it can be used in the preliminary phases.

For finishing, I prefer the reliable if rather slow orbital sander. They can be bought as power drill attachments, in which case the chuck of the drill has to be removed. You can also buy orbital sanders as separate self-powered units, of course. They have a light and cushioned touch which creates its own momentum, because all you have to do is hold the sander down and simply guide it along, not push it hard. It is practically impossible to overdo the job.

Lastly, you can use a power drill with a lambswool buffer, and this will put a gleam on any kind of surface, being particularly effective on oak or mahogany. Here again, the buffer must be kept on the move, especially if you are using wax polishes, otherwise the friction generated by a stationery buffer can cause burning and discolouration.

If you were to organise a poll and ask twenty people the purpose of the router, more than half of them would think it was something to do with traffic. Because of its fairly high price in comparison with other power tools, the router is not the kind of tool you see in every shop. I am always amazed, because it is one of the most versatile of all power tools and it warrants more publicity. As soon as I got my hands on a very well designed Stanley Bridges router, I inscribed my wife's name on a piece of wood and, only a few seconds later, after changing the cutter, I was fashioning an intricate dado which would probably have taken hours to do with a combination plane. I should mention that I had not up to that time used a router. It's as easy as that.

Routers are very simple in principle. All they consist of is a powerful electric motor in a stout casing, a means of fitting the cutter, and a jig inside which the cutter revolves at high speed. Stanley Bridges have now added a clip-on light which enables you to see exactly what you are doing and to work to even closer tolerances. By means of a threaded screw round the body of the router it is possible to raise or lower the cutter, varying the depth of the cut. The

A router should be balanced and fitted with two handles
for complete control and easy manipulation

other thing which a router has is a high-pitched whine and an ability to shoot out a stream of wood shavings, as a result of which you get the waste wood right down your shirt front and in your hair. I generally have a bath after using the router, wondering why the designers have not yet introduced a small deflector plate or chute to push the shavings elsewhere.

From what I have said you might imagine that the router is a very unpleasant tool to use, what with the noise and the shavings and the need to bend down to see what you are doing. However, it is a very satisfying implement. The cutters are precision tools, made for specific jobs, and a high degree of precision is possible, even for complicated jobs. It does exactly what you want it to do, because it rests on the wood and does not suffer from vibration or shakes. I do not know of any other tool capable of cutting a fluting as rapidly or of clearing the wood from recessed panels. At the moment I have a piece of English oak four feet square waiting to be carved as a crucifix in relief. If I were to start clearing the background by hand, it would take weeks, and by the time I started doing the actual carving, I would probably be fed up with the sight of the wood. But the router will do it in an hour or two. It will also do cove cutting, straight ridging, chamfering, V-grooving, core boxing and rabbeting. Due to the high speed at which it works and the sharpness of the cutters, it attacks both hard and soft woods with the same efficiency, and it will also work on certain metals and many different kinds of plastics. Thus, if

you happen to have a job which calls for the jointing
of solid plastic sheet to wood, the router will cut long
joints—a job which could not be done with any other
woodworking tools.

A word about safety precautions. On most models
the designers have gone to great pains to recess the on-
off switch, but it is often of the toggle type and
therefore apt to be knocked. After some use, it
becomes very easy to flick on and off. Due to the
rounded shape of the router casing, it is generally
located away from the twin handgrips, which are used
to guide it over the workpiece.

The next point to bear in mind is that the template
section of the router moves up and down on a threaded
screw which encircles the body of the tool, and so it
must be screwed up to its highest point to get at the
chuck arrangement. Because the tool runs at a very
high speed, it is essential that the cutting head is firmly
and securely tightened in position, otherwise an
accident might occur, because the cutter could fly
outwards and hit you in the eye. Or, of course, it might
shear off part of your ear. Using the built-in depth
gauge, you can measure the amount of cutting depth
required and screw down the template accordingly.
Some routers do not have a built-in depth gauge, and
so you use a rule, arriving at the correct depth by trial
and error.

Up to this point the router must not be connected to
the power supply. I am locating this warning at the
end of the description of the tool and its uses for

The router cutting head in relation to the workpiece when shaping wood

obvious reasons, because it should stick in your mind.

The router is now placed flat on the workpiece and the workpiece itself rests flat on the bench, if necessary with a couple of G-cramps to hold it firm. The circular template is made of polished steel to aid smooth movement. If possible, cutting should commence in an area of waste wood, where any early mistakes do not matter. Once you are satisfied with the depth adjustment and the machine is running at full speed, you can get on with it. The beauty of the router is that, due to this preset depth arrangement, it will not go on chewing into the wood. It cannot do so unless you move it, and so you can work at your own pace. A lot depends on the height at which you choose to work. I prefer the job to be at waist level, so the workpiece has to be blocked up. In the beginning, it is a good idea to take frequent rests until you get used to the high-pitched whining noise and the stream of shavings. I usually chalk out the guide lines on the wood, because they can be easily seen, and chalk is easier to remove than pencil.

Cutting angles and curves should also be practised. Most routers have a detachable fence for straight cutting and the lip of the fence overlaps the edge of the workpiece. But quite apart from that kind of aid, some freehand manipulation should be done. Many of those 'hand carved' house name plaques are rattled off with a router and then finished with conventional carving tools, although you would never think so to look at them. The router is also used extensively for fabricating display material for exhibitions and television studio sets. A wide range of interesting effects can be gained by using different types of cutters at various depths. In America several wood sculptors and other craftsmen have done very well for themselves by producing unusual panelling, using this method. It is an irony that a fibreglass moulding firm is using some of them as masters to mass-produce imitation wood panels.

While routers were until quite recently found only in the workshops of the professional cabinet maker and worker in wood, the standard tool has been modified and made somewhat lighter. An approximate price for a router to the following specification will, at the time of writing, be between £35 and £45: $\frac{3}{4}$ hp motor AC/DC Universal voltages 110, 200–250. Full load current 3·5 amps. Maximum cut in wood, $\frac{3}{4}$ in. diameter $\times \frac{1}{4}$ in. deep. Spindle speed no load 20,000 rpm; full load 10,000 rpm. Collets suit $\frac{1}{4}$ in. diameter shanks. Maximum vertical movement of spindle, 1 in. The adjustable fence allows for quick setting of work from 0 to $3\frac{5}{8}$ in. A circle cutting attachment for cutting holes, rings and blanks from $2\frac{1}{4}$ in. to 14 in., and extra long rods is obtainable. The running speed of the router is in the region of 18,000 rpm on average, and so depreciation of the motor can be fairly rapid, so it pays to have it serviced regularly.

You do not as a general rule buy cutters in a large range or quantity, but only as, and when, they are wanted. They are, in any case, fairly expensive, because they are made of tungsten carbide, the hardest metal. Something like 20 different kinds of cutters are available. It may be helpful to run through them and indicate their various capabilities.

V-grooving bits—used for lettering and sign work.

Straight bits, single flute—for general purpose routing (rabbeting, grooving, dadoing, etc.).

Shear cut bits (lefthand spiral)—down cutting action. Produces very smooth edges and is useful for grooving veneered work.

Shear cut bits (righthand spiral)—upcutting action. Lifts chips out of groove, permitting deep cuts to be made.

Veining double end bits—for decorative line work on any flat surface.

Core box bits, two flutes—effective for fluting flat surfaces (mantels and façades).

Rounding over bits, two flutes—for decorative edging and for dropleaf table joints.

Beading bits, two flutes—for decorative period furniture. Pilot guides router along edge of work.

Cove bits, two flutes—for decorative edging and for dropleaf table joints.

Chamfering bits, two flutes—for decorative edging and making concealed joints.

Dovetail bits—for making dovetails.

Soft metal cutting straight bits, single flute—for cutting soft metal, such as zinc and lead.

Spiral bit, right hand—for trimming aluminium.

Combination panel bits—these drill their own starting holes, and they are used for trimming
veneer and template panel routing.

Rabbeting bits, 1 in. shank depth—these are equipped with a pilot for making rabbeting cuts without the use of a router guide.

Long shank straight bits, single flute—for general
purpose routing where the nature of the cut re-
quires a longer shank extension.

Pilot panel bit—for trimming veneer and for template panel routing.

Bits for hinge mortising—fast cutting bit for making
mortises when the cut is started from the edge
of the work.

Straight deep cutting bit—for successively deeper
cuts in design work. Shank of bit acts as a
guide after the first cut is made.

Roman ogee bits—for decorative period furniture.
The pilot guides router along the edge of the
work.

Ogee bits—for decorative cuts. Clamp straight edge
or template on the work and use as a guide
for the outside edge of router edge.

Straight bits, two flutes, $\frac{1}{2}$ in. shank—for all general
purpose routing, such as rabbeting, grooving,
dadoing, etc.

Stair routing bits, $\frac{1}{2}$ in.—used to groove stair string-
ers for setting steps and risers.

A final word about routers. As I said earlier, perhaps the only difficulty is in seeing exactly what you are doing, due to the nature of the tool itself. Where edge working is concerned, however, the router can be inverted and bench mounted, but in view of the rapid speed of the motor, make sure that it is firmly clamped and bolted. The best way of bench mounting the router is to remove the template and mount the bit to the limit, which is generally about one inch. A fairly large hole should be cut in the bench top to allow easy access to the chuck. This done, a fence should be prepared, using wood and cutting a semi-circular shape so that the router bit is accessible from either side. By this means, the work can be slid along the fence so that the bit can do the cutting en route. But watch your fingers!

The power saw is not a specialist power tool, like the router. It is simply a handsaw 'in the round', so to speak, and its greatest virtue is that it is a great timesaver. It has not really been very much improved since it was first introduced, although the technical advances in the blades themselves have been considerable. This does not apply to all blades. There are some bad ones on the market.

The principle of the power saw is probably beyond improvement, because it is so simple. The saw itself is continuous, whether circular or in other forms. In the bandsaw it is flexible and it fits round the three guide wheels, one of which is driven by an electric motor or powered by means of a direct V-belt pulley drive. The trick of using the bandsaw lies in centring the saw itself on the wheels and getting just the right amount of tension in relation to the material to be sawn. Personally, I always prefer to work with a tight blade, but not because it saws any faster. When it comes to cutting on the curve, it is an altogether different story, because there has to be a certain amount of slackness to enable it to move round the curve, otherwise the blade may snap without warning with the two ends embedded deep in the cut. A good blade should take a

lot of punishment, despite its apparent delicacy, but
the cheaper ones, which are made from inferior steel
and badly butt welded, will generally snap if you so
much as look at them.

Proper bandsaw blades are sold at so much per foot
length, toothed and sharpened, and an average price is
30 p per foot, governed by width. However careful you
might be and however conversant with bandsawing
techniques, the inevitable kinks will always appear in
the blade, signalled by a light and regular clicking
sound as it passes through the guides. Naturally, it is
plain stupid to go on using a kinked blade, because it
might grow worse and the kink will probably mark the
sawn surface of the wood. As soon as the kink is heard
clicking, the blade should be taken off the machine and
the affected section laid on an improvised anvil and
lightly hammered flat. I am not claiming that this is
child's play. It isn't, because if you hammer it too
hard, it will flatten the teeth and may even fracture the
metal. This kind of rough and ready first-aid is
generally successful on blades up to half an inch wide,
but on the wider ones it is very difficult to do properly.

With all their prima donna temperaments—and no
two are alike—bandsaws are still capable of
performing some surprising feats. I have sawn intricate
shapes out of 3 in. English oak, yet the same blade has
snapped when cutting $\frac{1}{2}$ in. plywood. The physical
limitations of the tool are obvious, based as they are
on mathematical and geometric considerations. The
machine is built to a more or less triangular shape,

broken at one point for access to the blade and the sawing table. A triangle has an apex, of course, and it is this which creates the limitations. The one I use has a 13 in. neck, which is adequate for most work, but it would obviously be impossible to cut a 26 in. diameter circle on this particular machine. As with other power tools it is a matter of deciding how much use can be made of such a machine, because these are fairly expensive items, and to my mind the bandsaw does not possess the versatility of other power tools. On my machine you can tilt the table and secure it with wing nuts, and then cut a constant bevel. The other use which I have discovered is for bending wood, which is done by making a series of cuts to a depth of about 75 per cent on the reverse side of the wood. By this means you can bend a fairly stout piece of wood into a circle. It is possible to 'Swiss Roll' a thinner piece of wood, using the same technique.

Portable circular saws are useful, because they can be moved anywhere. The 26 in. size is probably the best. In carpentry shops they generally have a very large saw available. They will also have a big bandsaw, which is worked on the principle of the pitman wheel and a connecting rod which yields 1,000–1,200 strokes per minute, the stroke being up to 3 in. The amateur equivalent is the saw which gives about 1,400 saws per minute on timber up to one inch thick.

I mentioned the trouble in cutting 26 in. discs in wood. The best way of tackling the job is by using a

sabre saw. It is a simple tool, consisting of the motor
and a housing which incorporates the handle. There is
a crank action from the drive gear, creating a
reciprocal blade action of up to 3,300 up-and-down
movements per minute. The blade itself is only a few
inches long, and there are a variety of blades available
for different jobs. For instance, you can get a 7-teeth
for rough shaping; the 10-teeth for hard and soft
woods, and the 10-teeth type tapered for use on
plywood. Particular attention should be paid to the
method of fixing the saw to the rod, and I favour the
two-screw fitting, because the single-screw fitting
always stands a chance of failing or snapping from
metal fatigue. The tool is fitted with a shoe, by which
means the saw is kept flush with the workpiece. The
shoe is similar to the one you find on a sewing machine, but it is much larger. Most beginners simply jam
the saw into the wood and use brute force, which
results in the motor labouring and the blade buckling.
But if the shoe is first of all edged on to the surface,
with the saw at its highest point and not actually in
contact with the wood, it is safe to switch on and feed
the blade into the wood. The vital thing to do when
the saw is cutting is to keep the shoe flat. This may
sound easy, but it can be difficult, because even the
slightest tilt will throw the blade out of alignment,
causing an aberration. This is why the sabre saw will
not as a rule do intricate scroll work, for which a
bandsaw or fretsaw are best. In any case, sabre saw
blades are too wide for curlicues, although they are

very good for inside curves of a certain radius, especially when cutting plywood. Sabres will also cut ovals for you. The best way of doing this is to make a hole through which the saw will pass. This can be done in one of two ways—with the saw itself or some other tool, such as a keyhole saw. If the saw itself is used to make the starting hole, this can be done by tilting it so that the front prongs of the shoe enable you to point the saw at the wood, with the saw at its lowest point just touching the wood. The power is then switched on and the point should begin to nibble very gradually into the wood. As it goes deeper, the tool is tilted forwards until complete penetration is made. From then on, it is simply a matter of settling the saw in its usual position and working on.

At first sight, the sabre saw seems to suffer from limitations, because the saw itself moves up and down to pre-set limits. However, it can be adjusted to make a shallower cut if required by attaching wood shims to the shoe. The best way is to cut the shims of equal thickness and use as many as may be required. They can be attached to the shoe by means of a steel strap.

If you want versatility in sawing and other jobs, the radial arm saw is a very good choice, because it can literally do anything. The power unit is mounted on a steel column and overhead arm, and the unit can be moved along the arm on runners and then locked in position. The saw blade can be manipulated for cutting at angles. Radial arm saws are not as a rule on show in ordinary tool shops and so, if you are ordering by

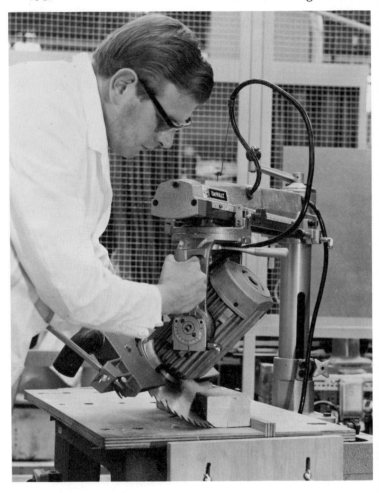

Radial arm saws can cut at any angle to fine tolerances,
providing all-round visibility in operation

post, it is as well to know what you are in for. There are two main types: the single arm in which the power unit and saw can be swung right round the column; and the second type is the double arm, which provides a much greater flexibility of manipulation. Regardless of the type, the circular saw is either 10 in. or 12 in., and has a speed of about 3,450 rpm. The power will be 1 hp, which is good enough for most types of work.

Radial arm saws are extremely versatile, capable of making all kinds of cuts (see diagram p 160). They can be used as sanders, using the drum type and, as this can be swivelled round to any angle, the advantages are obvious. It will also perform many of the router's jobs, again with manipulation.

However useful many of these power units may be, there is one in particular which has not lost its place and doubtless never will do. This is the common table saw, which can be used for bevel cutting, mitreing, ripping and crosscutting. With only a slight and simple adjustment, it will also cut many different mouldings. Some of the larger saw tables are fitted with two extensions to hold larger workpieces, and they are also fitted with attachments for measuring and guiding in addition to a fence to enable you to maintain a constant distance from the blade. Another is the mitre gauge, which runs parallel to the saw blade and can be fixed at any angle. This done, it is simply a matter of holding the wood firmly against it for repetition precision cutting. All saw tables are fitted with a guard which covers the top section. While this should be kept in position for the majority of jobs, there will be times when it has to be removed, especially when sawing large pieces of wood.

The method of holding the wood in position is

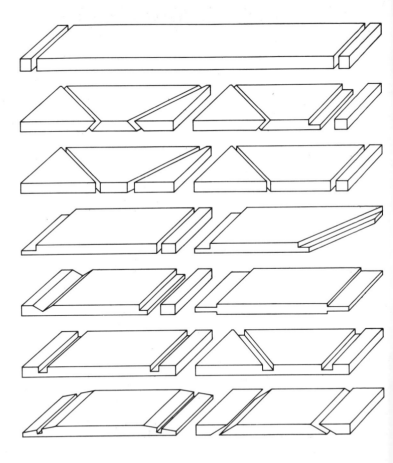

important. When it is a sizeable piece, you should hold it on both sides, keeping the hands as far away as possible from the blade. When it comes down to about six inches there is a fundamental rule that it should be held at only one end, because the saw has a tendency to snatch at it and try to force one side back into the blade in the last few seconds of cutting. This can be a very real danger to the hands.

13   Drill presses

A simple drill press is nothing more than a power drill mounted on a metal stand, which is equipped to raise and lower the drill to any level. Despite its simplicity, it can be quite useful, and it will carry out multiple boring operations to great standards of accuracy. In its professional form the press is fitted with its own power unit, and a variety of chucks can be fitted. In some models there are variable speed facilities. I have done a number of experimental dimensional 'carvings' and achieved interesting results not only with wood but also stone, plaster and semi-precious stones like malachite and North Wales slate.

There are plenty of good drill presses on the market, but I would not recommend the lighter ones, which are intended for amateur use. The very fact that they are so light is the basic fault, because the tool must withstand great pressures and carry a lot of weight in relation to its size. For that little bit extra you can buy an industrial drill press which will give many years of service. In recent years drill presses with a radial arm action have been introduced. This is, in fact, the type which I have used for carving and other rather unorthodox work. By this means you can cut grooves and hollow out shapes with speed and accuracy. It will also rebate, tongue and groove, and do even more complicated jobs, using the special cutting heads offered by CeKa Tools Limited of Pwllheli, North Wales.

The most important part of using the drill press is not the work itself but the setting up. First of all, the

Drill press with radial action

arm is raised to its fullest extent and the drill, burr or other tool is tightened in the chuck. The drills themselves are available in many different sizes and qualities, from $\frac{1}{16}$ to $\frac{3}{4}$ in. Consideration should be given to the nature of the material to be drilled in relation to the speed if the tool is fitted with a speed regulator. Without switching on, the drill head is lowered to the workpiece and the position checked. If a part-hole is to be drilled a depth gauge should be used. If the hole is to go straight through, the clearance under the workpiece should be checked. The drill head is then raised about one inch and the motor is started. As soon as it is running at the desired speed drilling can be done with the bit gradually engaging the workpiece. The regulating of the height is done by the metal arm which projects from the main body of the press. It is a matter of practice to know how much pressure to put on this, but the arm is fitted with a spring so that any relaxation of pressure will make it move upwards and the drill head will clear the workpiece. The first temptation is naturally to push the lever with some force, hoping that the drill head will somehow keep pace, but this results only in a loss of power and the motor will labour. A careful eye should be kept on progress, although a depth gauge attached to the shank of the drill is helpful.

Not long ago I did some interesting experiments with a drill press using a set of rotary milled files with ground teeth. These files used to be very expensive, costing from 50 p each, but a set of four can now be bought from some branches of Woolworths for as little as 75 p, and they are good enough for most jobs, even if they do have a short life and cannot be re-sharpened. Given a set of them it is possible to tackle an even wider variety of jobs than is possible with other power tools. Using a block of teak you can rough out and shape a free-form fruit bowl in about half-an-hour. This kind of job can be tackled with a radial type or single-position press. In the former the workpiece must be accurately and firmly screwed to the press table with the arm swung to and fro as required. In the latter the workpiece itself is manipulated underneath the fixed arm.

NOTES

NOTES

NOTES